VESNA KRMPOTIĆ

EYES
OF
ETERNITY

A Spiritual Autobiography

Translated by Lovett F. Edwards

NEW YORK AND LONDON

HARCOURT BRACE JOVANOVICH

Requests for permission to make copies
of any part of the work should be mailed to:
Permissions, Harcourt Brace Jovanovich, Inc.
757 Third Avenue, New York, N.Y. 10017

Printed in the United States of America

Library of Congress Cataloging in Publication Data

Krmpotić, Vesna, 1932-
Eyes of eternity.

Translation of Dijamantni faraon.
1. Krmpotić, Vesna, 1932- —Biography.
2. Krmpotić, Vesna, 1932- —Journeys. 3. Authors,
Croatian—20th century—Biography. I. Title.
PG1619.21.R63Z51413   891.8′2′15 [B]   78-23591
ISBN 0-15-129627-8
First edition

B C D E

HBJ

CONTENTS

My soul, I search for you within myself
As an unlit candle searches for its flame!
Diamond word, golden word, read me as
Your own thought!

EYES OF ETERNITY

*We shall become what we believe
and as much as we believe.*

Paraphrase of a Sufi poem

. . . Yes, I know the outcome already. But I cannot refrain from an attempt to alter it, though I know that I will not succeed in altering it. I know that I will not give up. From that effort emerges a mist which men call "beauty." So, because of that mist, I am involved in the travail of this writing.

All that I wish to know I have already known, once upon a time, but have forgotten. I believe that I knew it best in the beginning, as a flower knows how it will grow and in what hour it will open its petals. And all later life, for poets, is a struggle to remember how those petals open, how the flower becomes what it is. And in the end, if only I don't give up out of pain, perhaps I will once again penetrate to the beginning and become a flower which knows what it should know. But I will never reach farther than that starting point. Therefore I say: I know the outcome.

Meanwhile, from that bitter pain, from that struggle of memory and forgetfulness, something is added to the world. The world becomes uncertain because of that something, its eyes are filled with tears, it sneezes its way to recovery or disease. And out of that arises some breeze, some furrow on

3

the sea, something that won't give us peace for a moment. When that shudder is over, men breathe a sigh and say: It was beautiful. But while it lasts they hate it, turn their backs on it. Ah, beauty is a memorial to a catastrophe that has been happily overcome and yet might have cost us our lives.

Let me be free in these writings as I am free in verse. The same faith, the same doubt. Poets control their utterances as if they came of a dying race confined to a reservation; they become savages by permission. But as soon as they cross their frontier and become savages in the meadows of prose then everyone is astonished and upset. "Enough of this madness," they say, and set up a traffic sign counseling more moderate driving! *

Poets are chosen to disturb a world that without them would be complete (some would say: perfect). Without them, it might have been totally dark. It might have been perfectly bright. (If that ever could be established; for who

---

* Everyone knows that prose expression is not the same as prose and that poetry is not exclusively verse; even more than that, they know that prose can be expressed in verse and poetry expressed in prose. Everyone knows it so well that for a long time now there has been no one eccentric enough to try to convince us of it. Even so, how cruelly the poet interrupts his song when he blunders into unscanned prose! How, all of a sudden, he rejects the reasons by which he believes in poetry! How he becomes afraid of his savage, primeval thoughts when he is no longer within the stockade of his reservation! It helps him not at all to write "poetic prose"; for then he confesses a different logic of seeing, a different way of reading the signs of the times and tying the thread of things together—a stranger to himself to such an extent that it's as if his name signifies two persons. There is no visionary to whom that is odd. Let any such take his own verses and translate them into what they mean (or into what they do not mean) in terms of common sense—and he will obtain the most down-to-earth contradictions both of himself and of "common sense." How many times have I contradicted myself when writing about poetry; for I have not written about poetry in the same manner as I have written poetry itself.

could prove that Adam without Eve lived in darkness—or lived in light?) It doesn't matter. The poets are here and the world is no longer perfect. It began to swell up like the belly of a woman about to give birth, and, oh, the more it aches the more fruitful is the emptying of perfection. Pain is the measure of participation. For it, from our pain. Someone dug a well, completing the picture once begun, changing the shape of the continents, the slope of the earth's axis. And always, once again, let the serpent enter Paradise. What could a snake do in the earthly paradise other than push the world uphill, for it is allowed to enter so that one overripe fruit will again be set on the long path toward its bud. What could a poet do other than attack an innocent world with song which brings pain and awakening and an endless conflict with God?

Permit me, therefore, in my prose the same freedom as I have in verse: to describe with joy my partial forgetfulness of everything that is not that primal truth by which the flower opens its petals.

At the root of everything there is unsullied delight, so like a shudder. You can be driven mad by a simple pebble, not knowing if you are crushed or exalted. Everything is charged with monstrous life, every object lives possessed by a fury that will consume us as soon as we are aware of it; that will burn us up as soon as we recognize it. Ah, we alone are mortal in this universe; flaws in the clarity of crystal.

Ask me nothing, do not look on me so blindly; between us are words, like mist. Dear words, how I hate you! A being with five, six, seven senses created you, to give names to the fivefold, the sevenfold world. But when that being ventures into a reality that belongs to the eighth sense, then words can only destroy any later attempt at the reincarnation of that same reality. For "from there the word returns, its task

5

fulfilled." * What else can then be done except to stammer like a man drunk or spellbound, shrieking out: "Wings! Wings!" like Tin Vasionac, or rasp like a singer of the ancient Vedas intoxicated by soma: "Oy, hoy! I am drunk!"

But since I am not able to keep silent, then at least I will tell fairy tales, haikus, riddles, jests. Listen to me, forget all they taught you, for they taught you sterile formulas and impotent facts, whereas all real knowledge was within you from the beginning. Knowledge of things you regarded as arcane and ignorance of things you thought were clear to you. Don't go far from the answer which you never had to learn; now you must learn how to entrust yourself to it again, how to dig it up from underneath the corpses of others' thoughts. Listen to me and forget all the learned stupidities under which they kept burying you, and recall that which you already know. How much labor and effort is needed for you to turn from the outside to the inside, and how slow and painful your advance in that unaccustomed direction!

What I want to grasp, together with you, is too simple, so simple that perhaps it cannot be grasped. Therefore I am imagining the more complex world of fairy tale; I am sketching the firebird of Manipur, that jewel city. These things are all toys, to force mind and imagination to begin to play, and game by game to be lured into an unknown land where they will be transformed into that about which they think and about which they dream.

Therefore I build Manipur, I surround it with a moat of vipers, and above the moat, as you can see, floats a bridge of dead ravens. Thus I create, intangible and invisible, my city of refuge. Then, too, I plant golden saplings in blood and summon scarabs and moths to a banquet. I rummage among the bones of ancestors and in the mouths of far-distant kin, with a twofold mask I rummage—at one end to

* From the *Shukle Yajur-Veda*

6

write learned Chaldean books, at the other to disinter them from the sand and to labor over them. But what I am searching for is so unhidden that it could be hidden, that it could be open, that it could be mastered, that it could be lost. Ah me, what I search for, what you search for . . . cannot be possessed, cannot be seen, cannot be understood; but it can exist.

Under the blind white coat of wash is a vast living fresco —an unknown sight. I will not say that it has existed "from time immemorial" or that it "grew step by step," for its time is not my time and so is immeasurable by my measures. But that sight has a meaning that calls on me incessantly to liberate it. Writing is an attempt to begin rubbing somewhere on that white covering. What first appears will not be clear, nor will it illumine us; we will not distinguish whether it is a part of the beginning or the middle, if it is a detail of some collective scene, whether it is a lost color, whether it is a fragment of a portrait or a landscape. We have no idea what lies under the coat of wash! What courage we need to go on with the scraping! For "not a few perish at our work." * We fear that we are not ready yet for the revelation awaiting us. That its pure joy, so like terror, will not consume us in its flames.

Just two or three more inches of the fresco and we will fall exhausted. Just two or three light-years and we will end up in the womb of the mastaba, alongside Pharaoh's treasure. And then, we will have the freed part of the picture stretched on a canvas of modest dimension. For who can see oneself whole and go on living afterward?

* *Rosarium Philosophorum: Nonulli perierunt in opere nostro.*

7

THE MISTRESS OF THE GREEN ISLAND

What am I doing here, between the slowly
moldering sculptures of the Nile and the locks of the
sadhus which writhe and strike at me on the banks
of the Ganges? I am delving deeper, deeper into
my own distintegration. That is what I am doing.

For two years now I have been living on an island in the Nile. The Circe of that island has long, moist green hair; she tests her innocent spells on the inhabitants of the island. For example, none of us islanders can see that she lives on the island or that this has to do with a single river that closely embraces us in its brown, muscular arms. Only when we climb to the top of the tall tower that juts out from the male south do we catch sight in the distance of the strong trunk of the Nile, not yet divided into two lesser branches that will later entwine about our tiny green nest. And again, somewhere to the north, we see where these two branches once more merge and move toward their foliate capital, which supports the Mediterranean.

In the fork of that trunk, then, Circe has her dwelling.

I have settled down on the island no less comfortably than she. When I had convinced myself that everything about me was harmless, I began to unburden myself of my memories. In no special order, like a truck that brings building material. As it comes, so it is unloaded. One whispers: "Aha, here

I am in Egypt." Egypt is certainly a suitable soil on which to unload memories, though I don't know why. Perhaps the memories know, since they pour out so tumultuously.

Signs of some secret, almost extinct, understanding between me and the proprietor of this greenery soon began to appear; my children grew as if rushing up a staircase, their shadows danced on the muddy hide of the river. A petty anarchy broke out regularly, over the weeks, over the months. I had experienced this in the past, had lived through its charm when they fell asleep, tired and satiated. That family rhythm brought me peace, allowed me to delve into myself with greater dedication, even though I did so in strange, acrobatic postures; between two questions my children asked, three during lunch, thirteenfold at supper.

So we lived on that Bujan, on that Avalon. One day my husband asked if I wanted to stay or go. I smiled vaguely, for much the same thought had occurred to me. "As you wish," I said in reply. "We can sail away or we can stay; just as you wish." As I said that, I stared into the green-tressed twilight to see what Circe would do. But it was as if she had not heard. As if it were all one to her.

Clearly I was expecting to be bewitched. What was our landlady doing, little mother Mokosh, who had been working for us over the past two years; was she cooking something from the bitter herbs of the Nile? I hoped that she would transform me into something different, no matter what. For the human shape had begun to irk me unbearably. I expected that she would do that much for me, if for no other reason than because of our age-old Adriatic malice, because of the potion of Lošinj seaweed that had been of such fatal attraction for the comrades of Odysseus. But there was nothing; Circe remained silent, did not move a finger. I was bewildered, and a little offended.

Until one day—and now I am not sure if that day had not preceded all the other days, that it was not perhaps the first day after our disembarkation—right up to that day I had not seen the trophy hung above the entrance to her lair. Cow's horns and between them a suspended moon. I understood: that was my former skin. Circe had clearly, and in no way innocently, transformed me into a woman.

Cow's horns and between them a full moon in three colors, the three-in-one goddess who binds all that is loosed and looses all that is bound . . . the past which that treacherous snake had taken from me. I walked between my two children, everything was the same, everything was peaceful. That is why she allowed me to go. That is why she did not allow me to go. Now and again, at night, my eyes would fill with tears and I would see through the green mist over the Nile the glistening horns. Circe, little mother of Sycorax, was boiling her salamanders there on a submarine fire. Silver, my silver, glistened there over that labor and good men stumbled there in the darkness. Now and again, at night, I would hear the gong of the full moon as it moaned in the temple on another island—Philae.

Calmly, as if nothing had happened, I unloaded my burden. The stones crunched like the brittle bones of a plowed graveyard. How many had been buried there, I asked myself. Sometimes it seemed to me that I recognized extinct forms from ages before Circe, when the islands of the Adriatic and the Nile had still not risen to the surface under the sun. My recollection began to unfold like a snake spawned before the deluge. Shudders slid down its coils and shudders slipped down my own spine. Shudder after shudder, one merging with another, until they formed a fantastic pattern on the body of the great Kundalina. The slumbering spiral awoke and sank into itself. O, how deep is the memory of our race! No one believes that we are so old, but when they come to saw into the trunk, in the saw cut they can catch sight of the rings, the dizzy whirlpool of the ages! The trunk collapses into the whirlpool, into the coils of the snake Kundalina—collapses toward its central point, toward its root and the bud of its growth.

Sometimes it seems to me that I recognize in the depths of the spiral a dull gleam. Who is there? Who is it that sends me signals from below? What sort of galaxy appears at the end of the world? The gleaming reflection of some golden fleece? Is it the jewel of the snake, the sapphire of the moon? Is it *alatir* or *chintamani*, is it that philosophers' stone by which I shall come to understand that only in this place can be found everything that has been lost in other places? I dug into, I bit through, layers of darkness, suspecting that to be the only way to destroy Circe. Suspecting, all along, that I'm spewing out ages of fossils while searching for my own embryo, while searching for that which was wiser than anything that eventually grew out of it. Calmly, as if nothing were happening, and yet everything was happening.

Thus it was on that island, on that Ogygia, in that Elfland, as it always is. Only I cannot tell when all that began. For whoever sips of Circe's draught, in him past and future are tangled. He begins to ascend and to descend at the same time and looks with astonishment at his motionless face in the turbid mirror of the Nile.

The enchantment that husked from me my Isis nature . . . left me at peace to adumbrate the way of descent into the womb of my race. For a man does not delve into himself for fun but because he hopes that by so doing he will discover his own image that has been taken from him and now hangs as a decoration on the doorpost of a witch's kitchen.

THE GIFT OF TONGUES

I do not deserve your belief in me
until I once more become what I sing.

I was born thirty-seven years ago. Is birth that beginning which I am trying to evoke? If it is not, then certainly it is a turning point in the story of my life, the moment when the judgment of eternity washed its hands of me. From that moment I became the accused who, now more rapidly, now more slowly, advanced toward his punishment.

In the beginning it was loveliest of all. Things co-operated with me as never before. Every shape seen for the first time "responded." The sound that I heard before grownups told me the name of the unknown object remained its secret name, a password by which that object answered me. It merged with its appearance as skin with a face. Yes, every object had its own peculiar appearance, its own unique sound; nor was it possible to deceive it by using a strange name.

Today I reflect on why it was that things responded to me by their right names. Probably because I had complete faith in them. Grown-up sounds at that time were alien to me—the words of a language that was not my mother tongue, a language that one "made use of" but did not speak. I watched with delight how objects, as soon as they could, withdrew into their shells whenever some alien grown-up

12

words touched them. And I at once pronounced the real word, in their mother tongue, and the shapes dissolved and led me into their home, among their closest kin.

I don't know when we first began to draw apart. As I grew older, the sounds grew fainter. Something had frightened them, some insensitivity on my part which sprang up and led me into the deaf world of grownups. I don't know if I noticed that at the time, but the things certainly knew well what was happening. I learned better and better that language which was not mine alone, and as a punishment that gift of tongues forsook me. It fled away, surrendering me to a deaf guide in a glass forest. But I cannot forget its singing; I mimic it in my poems; and it, the offended siren, from time to time turns to me and echoes them with laughter.

I ran, my boots wet with dew, through a morning meadow, like a theme coursing through a symphony. I never asked anyone about my kingdom of sounds. It seemed to me that I knew quite surely that no one else could hear what I was hearing. Then, too, there was no one so incomplete as to be humiliated by such a question. Apart from that, like all children of that age, I had not yet learned the bitter skill of translating the inner voices into an alien tongue.

Now and again it happened that I, spontaneously, under the pressure of my abundance, threw out some overseductive rhymes; then the grownups would gaze at me, worried and startled. I remember that event in connection with the pattern on a plate from which I had been eating in the baroque dining room of the Castle Park villa. It was a classic Meissen design with flower motifs. The pattern on the rim of the plate was arranged in four-four time—a bulb, a flower, the same flower inverted, a heart-shaped leaf. Each of those four shapes had a life of its own, with its own sound, movement, mood, and appearance. I heard the first motif pronouncing in a sluggish and ill-humored drawl the sound *leek* and become transformed into the face of a fat woman well advanced in years who turned and replied in some embarrassment to a child's question; a frown was gathering between her eyes as if her shoes were pinching her. The second motif, a primitive flower, suddenly interrupted this theme of sluggish ill humor and developed swiftly and cheerfully like a fountain, echoing with a bell-like laugh and the full lips of a petal; that was *joy*. Behind that sound was an exclamation mark. Then my worried mother hastily looked down, her drawn Gothic face scarcely managing to check the mischievous little girl with the tiny, rounded face who was jumping up and down and waving. *Manners, manners*, that worried alto said. *Ovalencia*, shouted the little girl. The episode ended good-humoredly; the chin of some acquaintance of my mother's, or some aunt who had come on a summer visit, stimulated me to all that play of fantasy. *Come, come*, she said in a voice from somewhere in the background of the main street in Dubrovnik. Those sounds flowed in rapid rhythm: leek, joy!, manners, manners! come, come!

Over lunch and over supper those accents and all that went with them surged in my mind and rotated the blue Meissen on the yellow damask. When they became too tempestuous I let them flow out. "They're not without a certain sense," my father said, gazing at the design on his own plate.

> O omnipotence, O woe, woe,
> For through Thy pierced ears
> I little by little flow into silence.

In that villa on the Castle slopes, the edges of my being hesitated like the contours of a cloud. That edge was a ring of magic fire which as yet maintained no one within itself. I was still nobody. I still did not have a body. When I lay in the grass I was the grass, when I swam in the sea I was the sea. Armies of young Siegfrieds continually crossed the dividing line between me and the world.

I went in and went out as I wished in the green cellars of the plants, in shifts of mist, perfume, and shadow, and they one and all fitted me as if I had been poured into them—much better than the human skin in which they later imprisoned me.

I don't know when there was no longer a magic ring, when the cloud remained nailed to the heavens, when the fiery thorns stiffened around me. Outside, beyond the wire, there were still flowers, waves, the soughing winds. I received only two eyes, only two ears, only two nostrils, and words, lashings of words. Before, I had been an eye which looked at sight itself; before, I had been an ear which listened to sound itself; before, I had been a nose which flared at the perfumes; and I had had silence, the essence of communication. So I found myself bound in a close-fitting skin, buttoned to the crown of my head, an anaesthetized patient on an operating table, a patient unconscious of everything save pain. Pain ticked out the minutes, built into me like a clock in a tower; the muffled measures of my dark timelessness, the centuries of black Kali.

I don't know when all that took place, or, to put it better, was taking place. Gradually, like the red and yellow on the skin of an apple. Only: it happened, it was happening, it is still happening. Witness my longing to return to the kingdom of charmed speech. Witness my words which speak only of that return. Nothing else interests me. Nothing else do I love.

Therefore, with such Janus strides, I rush after beauty; to it, from it, to it, from it. For it is beauty that sows hope of a return and then at once uproots such hope. That is why it is so irresistible and so cruel. Beauty is a face that draws nearer from the world of freedom, senselessly draws nearer to the flaming barrier and leans against it, smiles and then flees down the meadows, on the track of dandelions, on the track of dandelions . . .

How can I follow? Thus, stretched out on a table under

15

dark floodlights, with numbed limbs and feeble, wakeful pain. After how many terrible thrusts of the scalpel will I again deserve the dandelion image . . . the hundredfold heads that live scattered over all the plants of the meadow and even over their own stems, freed of their burden.

FLOWER NOTES

*I am that part of the wind, of the flower, which has
been expelled from the wind, from the flower; and
as the wind slides over the flower, the flower
inhales for a moment its own perfume and for a
moment becomes the corolla of the world.*

The flower that I lure by my words . . . that whole flower
which I lure petal by petal, color by color . . . that flower,
that dandelion, my life . . . enters into me by the seventh
gate, never totally, never all at once. Through the gate of
ancient sight and smell, through the gate of lost touch, its
signals travel, red as roses, fragrant as jasmine, soft as a
pansy; one by one they swim into the insipid darkness of
my brain which swiftly patches them into an image, pastes
them on a background of memory. And before me waves the
flower, an eternal mystery.

I shall never know what a flower is until I see it from all
sides at once, till I can touch it from all sides at once, till
I can sniff its perfume at the same moment as I see it and
touch it. Ah, I shall never know what a flower is until I
myself once again become a flower, that flower which does
not know that it is a flower and, not knowing, is wholly
transformed into a blossom.

That flower which lures me . . . that moonflower on the
terrace overhanging the Nile, that lotus which I absorbed

from the hands of the Buddha Padmapani at Ajanta . . .
That flower which is the visible part of Flower, even as I
am the visible part of Myself.

The hot wind of a May afternoon pours out, a wind that
flows over the white-hot tableland of Mokatta and then sinks
over the craggy and dust-laden Arab Quarter, contorted like
the toenails of the giantess, the Citadella, who squats there,
barricaded in her self-forgetful stupor, then rises again over
the dead and gloomy housetops and then, charred by these
contacts, flies to the island in the Nile, swoops among the
flowers of the hanging gardens, is washed by them, and,
thus cleansed, casts itself into the Nile, a cheerful suicide.

How that wind caresses the moonflower . . . how the
moonflower returns its caresses . . . How all things caress
one another, mingle, merge into one another, each moment
losing their boundaries. Only I, firmly immured within myself, am impotent to go anywhere, to touch anything. Alone
before the flower, I implore it: Come out, flower, or whatever you are; show yourself to me, call to me! Thus the
snake charmer summons the snake from its hidden lair. For
the snake charmer knows the secret language of the snake,
knows its vibrations, knows the password to its organism.
Long, long ago, while still in the Castle Park, I forgot the
password to my flower.

Perhaps I could sit before the moonflower, write about it
to insanity. To write, that is, until the moonflower appears
before me, unable longer to resist me. There is an itch between my eyes, on the blind freckle of the third eye; thus
I at least know that I am blind; my sight realizes its lack
of sight.

I don't see it, for that flower grows in a space to which my
words don't reach—I "look" at it with words as a blind man
"looks" with his staff; he looks only at what is just before
his feet.

My words, when they are at their best, sense only the
direction of their flight, as a migrating bird heads for its

homeland. And that is all. For we are allowed to sense the region where our homeland lies, the goal of our desires, when we cannot fly to it.

To write until insanity on the face of a statue, on the body of Nephthys; until self-forgetfulness, to stroke with one's finger the outline of that body which writhes within me, a miniature Ouroboros; until that outline opens and allows me to enter, facing the supreme twins, sweetness and horror, the princess and the cripple, of this world.* Within, in the hall of the palace, where in the voice of angels the oath is taken that "there shall be no more time."

I am alone in front of the moonflower, dark with grief. The day is so radiant, so summery, the sky so vast and deep. Ah, all these are merely words: radiant, vast, deep . . . Vain words with which I summon those that bear them. Words are on my lips, but no one's kisses.

The flower sways before me like a keyhole, like a *aide-mémoire* to some inner chamber. Who has placed it there? Looking at it, gazing long at it, once again I ask myself why I was given the gift of reading signs and symbols and why I am not allowed to enter the hall where the ceremony they announce is taking place? Why this allurement? Is man only a transient form of a being to whom that third eye will be opened, the eye of Shiva, which looks into the noumenon? Now the signals tease him, that halfling; they itch on the marked spot of the future eye, just as the light stimulates the frontal spot of the blind worm.

---

* Before Innan and Eresh-kigal, twins: one rules the heavens and the other the realms beneath the earth.

Before Osiris and Set, twins: one rules the green and the other the desert.

Before Zeus and Hades, twins: one rules the heavens and the other the underworld.

Before Isis and Nephthys, twins: one rules life and the other death.

Before Baldur and Hoder, twins: one rules youth and the other old age.

Before myself and Myself, twins: one rules nonexistence and the other existence.

I am doomed forever to feel the insufficiency of this flower; I am condemned to search for its totality. I know that to find it means to find everything and to see it is to see everything. Man knows everything or nothing; either one moonflower or no flower at all.

The dandelion from a Dubrovnik garden, the lotus shining in the hands of the golden-faced Bodhisattva, the moonflower that sways in the breath of the Egyptian wind . . . all these are the petals of my Flower, the only one that liberates me from that part of me which is dead and drags me toward the grave.

BIRTHDAY

They hung me on Friday, by my own breath,
By a bloody rope.
A mask with golden eyes
Placed the noose around my neck.

By my breath, by a bloody rope!
Gaze on me, hanging, swaying.
On my dead skin I still feel
That burning golden eye.

It was on Friday, on Friday on the Gradac Hill;
They strangled me with a short breath,
With a rope
Which countless millions have greased.

The last I saw of life
Was the hangman, rocking and swaying down below,
His golden eyes following me
Through the dead gloom.

Only those staring eyes
Still gather what is left of me.
In their glint, like a golden fly,
My soul swoops toward the fire.

FIRST RECONNAISSANCE

The promised dewy unawareness is the morning
freed of my own eyes.

The story, therefore, begins with my guilt and with my scream of disappointment at the unreal world to which they had condemned me. The first reconnaissance on that path to my punishment was beauty.

As soon as I became aware of myself, beauty pained me. The clouds pained me, the seas pained me, the Elfland scents of Lokrum pained me. Every brightness and charm could exist without me, just because it was bright and charming, for I was not a part of it, I was not needed in that bright and sweet part of the world.

The story, therefore, begins with the withering of that dewy unawareness. They pushed me to the beginning of the way; and the beginning of the path was the peak where I endured for a breathing space to salute the abyss that was being prepared for me. From those depths the heralds of the end flew toward me. Beauty was the first announcement of that ultimate punishment.

I recognized it through my increasing feeling of being forsaken. Something should have appeared and I, not knowing what it was all about, should have whispered to myself: "Aha, here it is! It's coming!" Who was that? What was that? Only later I heard that certain things are called beautiful. For example: a moving cloud. It poured out, far up in the skies, leaving me below on the earth, fettered in my five years of life. Then, too, in the crown of a stone pine would flutter the sound of the ships' sirens from the Little Harbor and there it would wander like a stray calf. Or under the arcades courteous conversations would flow, slowly like the sand in an antique hourglass. Were they really ships, was it really rosemary, were they really birds of passage? No, it was a Voice which called me Somewhere, but I couldn't break out of my shell, out of that high thorn-wreathed tower.

On the summit of the hill Svarožić's cloak quivered, glinting golden. "I am coming!" I cried out. "I am coming!" I shrieked. O my God, I don't ask where, nor do I ask who calls me; I must break out of my shell, out of the strong thorn-wreathed tower.

What is the cloud to me, the murmur of pines, the perfume of the lands that smolder in the slow, painful lanterns of the lighthouses? They don't make me forget myself; on the other hand they recall me to myself as to some incurable malady. I have seen men who seemed as if they were drunk in front of some object or some sight; devoted to it, lost to themselves. Then I, envious, would imitate them. I would smile blissfully or frown blissfully, whispering: "How lovely!" But in fact I would feel within myself: "How cruel!"

So I don't know what is beauty; I don't even know what is ugliness. I recognize only what recalls to me my banishment to this flesh. So I pass by these signposts, collecting only their names, vain fetishes of the real sounds—Lokrum, roses, waves, Charlton Heston, Nanga Parbat, the moonflower in the wind. . . . Not one of them has mercy on me, not one has ever swept the differences between us.

HELL

*If there is a heavenly kingdom, then there is Satan's
kingdom also: it is within us, within us.*

From my tenth to twentieth year I lived in hell. To be more
precise, I was a hell to myself. The world about me was a
paradise which I was unable to enter; truly I was "an animal
goaded into itself as into death."

I grew up under the spiritual and material guidance of my
parents, tended like a plant in a nursery. We vagabonded
northward till at last we settled in Zagreb. Then the war
came to an end; once more we went regularly to school, the
air-raid siren in Petrinjska Street was silent. The war came
to an end; the world was touchingly new and sure of itself.
Yes, but it might well have been the other way around; the
world might have been stinking carrion, fattening maggots.
I would have been no more unhappy for that. On the contrary, I would have felt better for it, because it is better when
you are convinced that responsibility for your fate is not in
your own hands. Therefore the days of smog before winter
came hurt less than the amber days of approaching spring;
they proffered themselves, good Samaritans, as a reason for
my hell. A reason, or at least an accomplice.

Hell surged out of my depths with quiet and inexplicable
force. I suffered as a sick man on his deathbed suffers, from

minute to minute. I squandered all my strength just to endure life; others lived it. To endure, to endure, that was the problem; another morning, another afternoon, another evening, and then to sink into a dream which for a short respite freed me from torment. And after that short breathing space once again to survive the spears of hateful light which penetrated my eyelids and restored me to the strait jacket of existence. Every morning I would flap and gasp like a whale in a pool of water.

Early youth is often a time of hopelessness—wherever it may be, in whatever circumstances. For circumstances are what we are ourselves. Only too often youth is a dangerous time when we are most ready to identify ourselves with our own suffering, to identify ourselves to such an extent that nothing remains of us apart from that undefined pain, our blind "I."

The years fell like leaden balls in a vacuum; with the speed of a feather. Suffering made me eccentric and unacceptable to those of my own age. Instinctively I strove to hide. That suffering was the abyss of my being from which I tried convulsively to drag myself. My fellow students observed with scorn my wretched, clumsy attempts to draw closer to them. I yearned for them, I yearned no less than I would yearn later for some Gösta Berling from the same summer resort. I valued too highly the company of those of my own age to know how to approach them, to be pleasant to them. I played the part of some second self, for a certain time even to myself; I filled diaries with imaginary torments, only so that I should not have to put a name to that one true torment which I concealed like an ugly wound. But it revealed itself through my feeling of being branded and lonely. As if I offered to my fellow students a ball to throw at that hidden wound. And it drew their blows.

Naturally, Someone or Something must liberate me. Something or Someone must come and take me away, free me from that "no man's land." I knew that somewhere breathed my native kingdom, which I myself had frittered away, without even noticing when I had done so, or why.

The years fell like leaden balls in a vacuum. More and more certainly I awaited my savior. I did not dream of "love," I dreamed of resurrection. My imaginary lover was not a fellow sufferer of my body but a ministering angel. He was the gentleness and the strength that would touch me, so that the pitch into which I had been cast alive would fall from me.

On how many innocent faces did I hang my expectation! On faces innocent of such a role, faces that would become frightened and disgusted at the abnormal hopes that led me to them. Luckily, not one of them got to know what I expected of them, for by inborn instinct I behaved "normally." Nevertheless, they sniffed out that within I was distorted by suffering and they withdrew from me as from a cripple.

I remember endless walks on terrible Sundays; watching from ambush as I at every step awaited my redeeming miracle. Appear to me in the semblance of a man, in the semblance of a man, in the semblance of a man, I implored more and more shamelessly. I expected, therefore, that He would recognize me at once and that He would approach me without introduction or hesitation, for He was born to redeem me, as I was born to be redeemed by Him. Existence really went on from moment to moment, from breath to breath, in an unendurable waiting for life.

The years fell like leaden balls in a vacuum. What was happening, what had happened, could be compared to the great hunger of a carnivore to which only grass is offered. Slowly, very warily, I began to eat grass. I felt better, even though the taste of grass was repulsive and made me vomit. But the terrible hunger cramps ceased.

A carnivore which, by force of circumstances, became a herbivore; that is what I became in the flock of my loves, the flock of my yearning, though it was all the same to me; grass was grass, everywhere it was tasteless and revolting.

For that reason I found it very interesting to try to listen to that unquenched hunger, lusting for other food, which hummed and sizzled inaudibly in the caverns of my body.

That hunger waxed and waned. Gradually, very gradually, it turned in upon itself and bit its own tail. It no longer stuck out from me as the hand of a drowning man from the water; slowly, within myself, I clasped hands with my savior. Far, O far distant, was the path to the moment when I would be able to look at those always absent eyes and calmly assert: *"You and I are pure. It is all the same."*

THE FAIRY KING'S VEIL

*Love . . . that unattainable something to which we
are loyal and because of which we desert beloved
bodies, deceiving them shamefully with their souls.*

Later I embraced everything with a mad desire to envelop
it entirely in my arms, so that the best part of it stretched
into a region where human hands could not reach.

There, all was song. There, too, was song. Is that where
the wound at the heart of every human love comes from?
We always embrace the angel's robe, never his celestial body.

All my loves suffered from the same malady. Always I
would embrace the fairy robe, sewn, it is true, according to
fairy measures. But in my arms it crumpled and became a
rag.*

* All these dear ones, silver and gold,
  From the hands of the Goldsmith, flying upward like sparks,
  Wither and die on my bare skin.
  All these dear ones are only robes
  Woven to thy measure, O Love,
  O bodiless Love.
  The robes which I wore, the robes which I cast off,
  All these, strong as pillars,
  Crumple at the moment I embrace them,
  When I, despairingly, want to touch with my hand
  The bodiless model which abandons them.

I watered it with tears, I watered it with tears, till it became dirty and slimy as frog skin. Nevertheless, that revulsion was the one thing remaining of my noble effort to live above myself; that revulsion was the only real memory of my flight into the realm of angels.

SOBER REFLECTIONS

I have nothing save my life, which is too tiny for silence and too vast for a tale.

My tentacles, stretched out into the past, are rigid and barren antennae, which in their groping can touch only what is like to them. And almost nothing in our experience, whether rigid or stable, disintegrates at the first touch of the probing, glinting scalpel, shifts through the garden of remembrance like a wisp of fog, slips away under the floodlights of consciousness like a coelacanth in the depths.

The past is living and constantly changing; it is called the present.

Which of our experiences is not a mad charge in several directions at once? What is not persistently renewed in many of our pasts, in many of our futures? But we believe only in small quantities of ourselves; a drop in the palm and not in a great Protean ocean. In any attempt at confrontation, such as this one of mine, we only carve ourselves out of our totality. Most often we carve according to a premeditated pattern, ready for anything, only to prove that we are what we are not. Yes, we oppress ourselves more and worse than anyone else can oppress us.

It is easier to understand sin than to acknowledge it. To penetrate into one's own experience is more adventuresome than any adventure. We thwart ourselves in that endeavor, fearing some unpleasant confrontation. We choose our recollections in some strange order more or less cunningly, preferring those on the fringe, those that have dried up like a scab.

I venture to cut into myself in those places where I expect the flesh will be sufficiently shallow and pliant. But even the most innocent recollections are waiting to swallow my scalpel, handle and all, even the hand that grips it, the whole arm up to the elbow and the shoulder. . . . Like something always living and hungry, the masked flesh-eating flower spreads as I watch . . . bringing a foretaste of terror, so similar to joy.

Every halt, every viewpoint, has its own inevitable dislocation. My glance into the past would be different were it not cast from the ramparts of this marriage. Or if I were not surrounded by the redoubts of two children.

Were I now unmarried, or divorced, my choice of the past would be different. For the backward glance always seeks for what contradicts the present situation, searches for some counterpoise, for what cuts across it at right angles, from height to breadth, thus creating the beginning of some coherent shape.

Married, buttressed by two children, I probably pay heed to the spray of the fountain and not its crystal jet: only the spray that the wind catches. Or, to put it differently and once again by a similarly inadequate comparison: today I am more inclined to the perfume than the flower. Were I unmarried, if I had no children, the flower would be more prominent than its perfume and the crystal jet would be more needful to me than the spray.

Finally, it is hard to say which love is which. It is hard not to mingle them in speech when they are so hopelessly mingled in reality. We start one love looking back; the other we overtake before it has begun. One we fulfill with another player; the other we resurrect with the tenth that comes to hand. One we want to kiss, but we find we kiss another. In short, we love one only through others; probably in a similar way we hate.

And then: *When* did something happen? *When* were we aware of a certain scene, a certain face? Has not everything several facets of its present, as a diamond has several facets of its brilliance? The eye loves by remembrance, as do the lips; and the future is involved in even the most immediate moment. The thing, the scene, is caught between glances— where is it? *

* A picture emerges from the depth of mingled colors; it becomes more and more taut, like a sail filled by the evening breeze. All that made it possible and everything that resulted from it was a darkening before and after the performance—it alone jutted out like an accursed mast, without bow or rudder, divorced from the chain of cause and effect. That picture was the rose-tinted Place de la Concorde, a place like a heart under a giant lens; I came to the surface in an evening of early May in that vast rosiness, tiny and deaf as one of many millions of blood cells which in its circular visiting of the universe once again wanders through the purlieus of the heart.

Someone from above threw a pebble and at the spot from which the ripples spread rose the needle of an obelisk; the disturbed ripples, the garlands of automobiles, quivered and melted between the houses into the evening.

And that face, which led me, very slowly, as if in a dream, from Zagreb, from the gloomy little editorial office on the fourth floor, to this beginning scene, now half blossomed like a picture of which it formed a part. I did not look at it but I felt little twitches of awareness under my skin.

Yet now, seen once more, gazing again at that nerve center of Paris, examining its lines and rearranging its unparalleled geometry, I realize that at that time I had not really seen it as I should. Then I saw only my own and another's transformation in that scene. Is that the reason why the Place de la Concorde now comes to the surface—its desire to be finally recognized?

What did I see that early evening when I emerged from the entrails of the Métro and ascended to the amber dome of the Concorde, into the flesh of a fruit at the height of its ripeness? Perhaps only the

Every glance is a glance of creation, every glance reveals the only possible order. Who could number all of them? They are driven simultaneously into the fortune-telling crystal of some object, some face, some event. But we trust only one of those glances. How little of ourselves we catch!

I write these sober reflections as an imaginary dialogue with an intelligent acquaintance, "a sober, bucolic reader." I have hung his picture on the wall in the frame of a barometer. When he frowns in disapproval, I feel contentment with the way I write.

For example, my disconnected narrative worries him, the trespass of myself into my writing; to him it seems that I am talking incoherent nonsense rather than maintaining the creative irrelevance of chronology.

He doesn't know the effort it takes to break the habit of regarding things in some artificial continuum such as time or someone's name-and-surname. The need to create such a continuum is partly, perhaps, inspired by fear, and partly made possible by the laziness of my attention. For any experience, every experience, that we are convinced is complete in itself, proves on more persistent analysis to be broken into differing, glittering particles mutually far distant one from another, as are stars in the universe. Every particle has its own rhythm and its own specific weight, the unrepeatable formula of its substance. But one glance cannot perceive all these points except in continuity and unanimity.*

---

announcement of a scene? Or perhaps its end, the heel of a flight whose beginning will soon happen?

* From the depths of blended faces arises an olive oval and in it two flawed greenish eyes, two green almonds. That is Georgia, "the divine Amazon," my friend over long years. So everyone says, and we two also. But, thinking it over, repeating that phrase aloud—my friend over long years—what do I do but equate all those millions of disparate little stars that twinkle on the region designated "Georgia." We are friends, naturally, and the best of friends; she has no better friend

Therefore, dear face on the wall, I will not write any "biography," I will not indicate any sense of direction, I will not follow the mechanical law of external continuity. To tell a story in such a way means forcibly to rip a single thread from the weave.

When you rip it out, it is a thread; when it is in the weave it is no longer a thread. Who knows what it is then—perhaps only a color or a point that appears and disappears in the design. . . . You draw it out of the weave, patiently tease it with a needle, and it shows that it is neither color nor pulse in the rhythm of the pattern. Only a meager little thread.

---

than I, nor I better than she. Nonetheless our friendship existed only at moments; at other, later, moments we lived one with the other simply from memories of those "friendly moments"—though even then we knew the sense of not-loving one another or were bored with one another. I want to say: most of all we gladly recognized that particle which flickered with the rhythm of "friendship" even though that particle was not the most frequent. But it was the most appropriate, as a fulcrum, something of which we were always aware.

Our graph in that continuum began in 1952, when we got to know one another in our first year as students of psychology. That was seventeen years ago—indeed, in our mutual field, there flickered past us millions of particles, a beautiful little galaxy. In recent times we have seen one another very rarely, since we live in different cities, even on different continents. But at that time we exhausted every morning, afternoon, and evening, every night. We were masters as consoling one another whenever our distress exceeded a reasonable measure, and were equally skillful in spurring one another on when our spirits were flagging. In short, we helped one another to live. After such routine actions we knew how to sit and ruminate on the experiences we had gone through together and overcome together. It was a symbiosis which not a single jealous overseer, either hers or mine, was able to demolish. Moreover, anyone involved with either one of us was in a way involved with the other without even being aware of it.

However, despite all that "continuum" truth about our mutual ties, we were friendly only occasionally—at moments. There were days, hours, when we treacherously waged war on one another; there were periods of indifference, of malice, of habit, of gratitude. Then once more would flicker that salutary particle of friendship, that unerring sense of intellectual and emotional unity.

How then write anything in the manner of a biography? A presumptuous question; it sounds presumptuous even with an exclamation mark at the end, when it is filled with amazement and pusillanimity. Biographies are always fakes. It would be better to ask: How should they not be written? What to avoid to prevent them appearing as fakes?

I would say that one should not follow the discipline of chronology, which enjoins a name, an event, a cluster of events. Yes, I am sure that one should not try to find an evolutionary trend, for such a trend does not exist; there exists only a spiral approximation or aberration from the mean. One should not avoid contradictions. Are we not such that paradox tells us most of all?

One should preserve oneself from what has been attained. In a self-recognized effort that is called: conclusion, formula. Attainment—what is it? Isn't it a disguised moment of defeatism, the moment when we take shelter in some system, escaping from loneliness? Before collapse? But that isn't a man's aim; his aim is not, while running away from probable disaster, to rot in prison, where he can only exist. Man's aim is to be free. Not to enslave himself to attainment, but to drive it unceasingly before him, like a scarab its ball of sun; continually to disinherit his work; to remain untouched by that; to be just as deserving of it as a fruit tree is deserving of its fruit.

Man's aim is: by resisting himself to attain Himself.

Therefore, I cast myself in various directions toward what I suspect to be the mean; so that every time I illuminate another past it is with a different weave. It doesn't matter that these pictures do not coincide. Let them devour one another.* I have no time for their so-called discords. Dear face on the wall, that is now your worry.

Writing of something long (or not so long) past, we, albeit

---

* Breathing has every moment another name and another form—now a panting, now a deep inhalation before roses, now the holding of the breath in a kiss, now a death rattle, now a slow outpouring. And yet it is still a uniform process; the disposal of the life-giving element.

inadvertently, stimulate the past. For memories, faces among so many indiscernible, unselected, faces at which we have pointed in scorn, will return by devious ways to await us on our path. What we remember will remember us.

Therefore a man, trying to write truly and fully about his whole life, always selects what will unfold only in the future.

Thus, selecting from the past, do I, too, leap back into my own steps which flash to meet me? O unpredictable game, and we thought that it was possible to "flee" into the past!

ONE MORNING, LIGHT AS A MOONFLOWER

There was once a time when I valued only what I had achieved by pain. People, words. Pain was the only familiar path into the unknown. With it I felt more free from pain than with any kind of pleasure. With it I felt that I was *I*. Even though I blindly, continually, sought for joy.

Later, perhaps because I had drunk from the Nile, I began to forget my former faith. One morning, light as a moonflower, I looked at the clouds over Cairo; they had done nothing to be so light, so quiet, so steeped in thought. Without effort, without resistance, all that: to be a cloud.

My former assurance poured out, too; without resistance, without pain. And all things that had taken its place, painlessly, in my life and felt themselves alien there now easily became the best and only things that I dared to call my own.

There was a time when, I myself don't know how, complete poems, songs, fell into my lap without convulsions, without tumult. I had the feeling that they were not mine, that they were the prey of outsiders, and I waited with apprehension for the day when the real hunter would appear. Those songs were strange to me and therefore I didn't fully understand them. But I left them as they were—incomprehensible to me—for I didn't dare to change them, even as I wouldn't dare to misquote the thoughts of others.*

That morning, quiet as a cloud, I felt myself walking on air with joy. Without reason, without effort, I became joyful, I became *I*; embracing myself as "after a long sojourn in a foreign land."

---

* He who fettered me
  In revolt and impotence
  Now drains my suffering
  To complete the world.

I was nineteen years old and didn't know from where it had all come. I shrugged my shoulders, I let it stay, disturbed, cold toward the song, but not indifferent to the fact that some strange bird had laid that egg. I didn't even know what was being said in that verse. I was scared lest someone ask me what it meant. Then cautiously, very uncertainly, I showed it to others. To make matters worse, they praised it; then others, too, continued to laud it. It became "an anthology piece." With the same feeling of chill and guilt I read it at literary evenings, grew used to calling it my own, though I didn't look on it as my own. It was like a child whom only the mother knows to be a foundling. I waited for someone to appear and demand his own.

No one came. Afterward I wrote many "someone else's" verses. I learned how to classify them among those that "hurt," those that were "mine." I interspersed them in my books, striving to conceal their sinful origins. I didn't conceal them, but myself grew accustomed to them.

No one made himself known; there was no voice of any kind, whether without or within. Then, perhaps because I had drunk of the Nile, I became unsure; could I not recognize in these painless eccentricities something very ordinary and terribly familiar, something that had always been there, and was therefore invisible—like one's own heart? Perhaps because I had drunk of the Nile, I arose, intoxicated, and spoke ancient songs amid the prophetic murmur of the leaves. So I and these alien poems, those most my own, fell into one another's arms: we embraced one another rapturously as after a long separation.

THE WAYWARD TRAVELER

I asked my shoulders whom they were carrying,
but they would not talk to me, would not respond
to superfluous questions.

There was never a night train flashing by in the opposite
direction to that in which I was traveling when my whole
body, my nails, my hair, the clothes I was wearing were not
filled with pain; as when experiencing some irreparable loss.
For that most precious one, for whom I had been searching,
was lost at the moment when I finally resolved where He
was; in that train which was quickly lost in the opposing
night.

Lost at some provincial crossing on the Belgrade-Zagreb
line, usually on a winter's night that stank of sulphur, and
electric bulbs like boils broke out over its sickly skin. The
world lost—and he who had lost it had not even noticed.

Then the lighted train was lost in whistles and tiny snakes
of sparks. At once it became terribly clear to me that had
been my train and I was sitting in this one by mistake. For
that precious one, that person who was most precious to me
in my whole life, was suddenly lost in that train disappearing into the opposing night.

I knew that the festive golden morning was breaking
somewhere in the heart of the world and yet my body was
contorted with that pain and that loss. Our ship was slowly

entering the harbor of Limassol in Cyprus. Resolutely and somehow mockingly a luxury passenger liner, of some Italian line, I thought, was rushing toward the open sea. There was a crowd of bright-colored passengers on deck, many of whom waved rapturously without knowing to whom or to what they were waving—to the skies, to the ships, to the dolphins. Among that happy throng He, too, stood. I did not see Him for He does not let himself be seen, for He is always in trains rushing in the opposite direction, on the deck of ships leaving the harbor I am about to enter. Suddenly, in the midst of all that clear, transparent gold and wine which poured down from above on the waves upon which danced millions of tiny conch shells with newborn Aphrodites, I felt forsaken, as if lost in the Pannonian plain; once again I breathed the depressing sulphur of the wrong line.

Once that figure who eternally crosses my path came perilously near. It was on the platform at Chalisgaon, a railway stop that bore so vibrant a name that it would have better graced some marble lace of Shah Jehan than a tiny station lost in the depths of India. I was waiting for the night train to Bombay. It would take me a hundred kilometers or so westward, toward Ajanta. Those Indian nights, warm and sticky like the skin of a newborn child! The waiting passengers were sleeping in the cramped waiting room, some even on the platform under the humming neon lights. I walked among the sleepers, humming to myself. From my earliest days I have always felt more myself when among unfamiliar things—for then, finally, the things around me become unreal, and not only I. Those are the moments of rest. I rested, knowing that it was no longer I who rested—it was some puppet I had thrust onto the stage in my place, at great risk to the performance.

Like a noisy, brightly lit toy the Delhi Express, the counterpart of my own train, but going in the opposite direction, rushed into the station. The sleepy tea sellers mumbled under the carriage windows, but the windows remained closed. One man only stood cautiously on the steps of a first-class compartment, then stepped down just as cautiously, as if descending onto the soil of some unknown planet. He paused some distance away and I didn't see his face. I realized only that he was wearing clothes of European cut. I strolled along and looked at him. He, too, stood and looked at me. He and I were the only persons awake. Probably he wondered at seeing me so unreal, as in a dream among the drowsy heaps—like a dream generated by all those tired heads. And I became terribly aware that this was the occasion, the unique occasion . . . to find out for myself. Almost at the same moment, in some opposite corner of my brain, the alarm of my conscience sounded, warning me to let this occasion, *too*, pass, not to enter that seventh, forbidden, door.

The train shuddered. The man started and jumped onto the step. Slowly, disappointingly, the shining black train moved toward Delhi. At the same moment, as if uplifted by the same force, our two hands flew out in greeting and waved as long as we could see one another.

Was that a flash from some distant quasar; the last flicker of the dying light from a coachman's lantern? I withdrew from the possibility of finding out. It was unnecessary. Under the crust of the dark continent an organ resounded in diapason. I didn't need that organist. I needed violins. Unerringly I had awaited the moment to raise my hand too late.

And that gesture forked into two opposing hands, that moment which like a dark swaying sapling grew in eternal Chalisgaon. That is the moment in which we wave to our love. What beloved man in my life did not repeat that same scene? Everyone is that solitary traveler through Chalisgaon. To be quite explicit: his departure made him whole.

EVEN WHEN YOU ARE MOST MINE
MY YEARNING FOR YOU
TORMENTS ME EVEN MORE STRONGLY

Is the aim of love to teach us that the lover cannot quench our longing for him?

When he is there, as near as is humanly possible, our desire is to call to him more and more frantically: "Where are you? Where are you? Come to me!" For *whom* was my longing calling, since the one I longed for lay beside me, surrendered as a trusted sword in the hand of an enemy? Blind diver, did it not see him? It saw him, how well it saw him, but just the same it went on calling desperately for him. It saw him, it saw the sleeping sword which should have cut off its head. But it was dead, impotent: an object.

My desire shrieked and stretched out its arms. Was the lover only a window at which my longing waited for someone else? Was the lover only a herald bringing a message from a distant betrothed?

I leaned over his face as if over a shallow pool in which the pure face of the moon is reflected. Something held me back so that I could not raise my head and gaze upward; we are so built that we look only toward the reflection. Something still prevents me from raising my head—not even in memory—and looking upward where he who sends me all that fool's paradise glistens, doubtlessly to remind me of myself. Lovers were his symbols, his betrothal ring, his verses, his letter from a land upon which I have turned my back.

And when you have put the ring on your finger and raised his letter to your lips, what happens to your desire? Does it grow greater or does it weaken? Can a ring lessen that desire?

I don't long for Your tokens, I long for You.

Who was it who cried out so; was it Juliet, was it Héloïse? No, but was it some name from the calendar of saints—Catherine, Theresa, Rabija?

Like a tiny spring which no longer knows how to
                    quench thirst
You murmur beside me, thirst-quenching love;
Leaning over you, my lips reach beyond your limits,
Beyond your limits.

You are deceived from the moment when I set out to
                    meet you
For the farther I emerge from myself, the more you
                    lose your outlines
And like a tiny death mask you fall from some
                    dreadful face,
Some dreadful face.

With cries of horror I would turn to the mask
To give it love and restore it to life with kisses,
That my kisses, already infected, should not leave
                    wounds,
Deep wounds.

Now I see you were only the lure in the trap
From which, perhaps, we at one time escaped.
You deceived and I too deceived,
Let me kiss you for the last time.

Theseus. Kiss Theseus, Ariadne, before he turns into the

face of Dionysus; before it melts like the greasepaint on the face of an actor before the end of the play; before it reveals the features of the lord of the drama, the author who is the drama.

KRISHNA'S FLUTE

*That alone which I came to see has hidden itself
deep in my eyes, like the light by which I
looked at it.*

I am that deer in Kabir's song that rushes onward, enchanted
by the aroma of its own musk.

Where is He for whom I strode through the weeks at
Zagreb, whom I sailed to meet in the waters of the Mediterranean and the Indian Ocean, who continually evaded me
in the gardens of Dubrovnik, that furtive Krishna whose
flute called me from so many directions at the same time?
If I am not granted to meet him face to face, why, at least,
have I not seen his burning bush on the peak of Grihakuta,
a sulphurous column from the Delphic navel; why have I
not seen the place whence he keeps silent and speaks? That
voice in whose harmonies I grew like a sapling in the whirlpool of my rings, that voice which calls to me from Mala
Luka, from the clouds that always move away to some place
where I am not, which rings the changes of male voices singing of promised, dewy oblivion from all sides, except that
side from which I came . . . where is that Voice, where is
it rooted, in what soil I still haven't plowed?

There remains only one land unexcavated, unexplored;
and now while I am writing about it, my old presentiment

expressed in so many "alien" poems, I hear that Voice grow softer, like the voice of a man to whom one has been talking and who sees that you have understood what he has been saying all along. . . . Strange, so quiet it seems closer; yes, He is surely closer, much closer than I had thought. It, that Voice, is just around that bend. Its roots are there somewhere, too close for me to touch them; my own soul is that last layer from which it grows.

Yes, I am that deer in Kabir's poem that rushes on deceived by the scent of its own musk, convinced that somewhere far away the doe awaits it.

Eh, Krishna, Svarožić, how long have you been jesting with me! Beyond every garden turning, beyond every Zagreb corner, have I hunted your winged feet in flight. That was my voice, wasn't it, that cried out from human faces, from the names of distant lands? Fruitlessly, I searched for truth; going farther away from it, from my own hearth. In the wrong world, in the wrong place; for I am not in myself.

CONCLUSION TO AN APOLOGIA

A rose
Cannot
Pluck
Itself.

At my entreaty the flower said to me: "If you want to know
what a rose is, you must become a rose." Then it closed
before my eyes and left me alone with my doubts, with my
uneasy kin.

My kin asked me: "What part of experience do you leave
behind when you step out of its magic circle? How much
can you see of it when you look at it from the outside? How
much recollection are you able to retain in your pitted palm?"

Instead of giving them an answer, I replied to the flower:
"While a rose is a rose it does not know that it is a rose.
Later, it senses that it is a rose and begins to sketch petals
and to perfume the breeze, but mainly the way such things
are seen from the outside, from that space which kneels and
implores the rose."

For our life is in one world and our words about life in
another. What else do our words know except to number
the rose by its petals, divide it by seasons, fraction it by
grades of flowering? All those quantities are helpless before
the rose which pays no heed to them and remains silent.
What else can I do with my writing except to look at the

one-time rose with the eyes of one who plucks it, what else can I do except see its southern, eastern, and western aspect from this northern, unflowering viewpoint?

It is morning. I tell what I have dreamed, but the dream is disintegrating, growing thin in words that are powerless to renew its hallucinatory, illogical reality. It is morning, I tell my dream.

They ask me: "Haven't you forgotten what is most dream-like, infinite, and that cannot cross the outline of the magic circle, the line of awakening?"

O former rose that fades, calling upon your time of blossom. You pluck yourself by memory. Your palm, like a crude sieve, plunged into the heavy dew of your history, now longs for some firm substance and pours through it all the sap, the prophetic diamond, in which quivers the bloom of your life.

THE DARK SIDE OF THE SUN

Searching for eternity, I let the minutes slip by—no,
I didn't pass through them but by-passed them.
And now eternity has responded to me with days
that don't last, with minutes that flash only for a
moment and only for themselves, like heavy dew in
a dream of the dense jungle.

There was a time when I tried to find out what fear meant. I walked in graveyards by night, when the trees in the mist were like the conceits that come into the minds of the dead. There was no more suitable place than Mirogoj cemetery at midnight. We were students and we walked, four of us together, sometimes three, sometimes two, or I alone. We trod the snow in light shoes; the screech of the last Mirogoj streetcar left us, frozen, under the frosty chestnuts. But we ourselves were white-hot, like swords before their mystic tempering. We made our confessions to one another, and passionately hid our real selves behind those confessions. Fierce disbeliefs walked through the world at that time, bitter and defiant impieties which were no more than the obverse of our passionate faith.

At Kamniška Bistrica, in the high Alps, I set out one night into the forest deep in snow and black moonlight. "Tonight

I shall know what fear is," I told myself aloud, threatening someone. I scrambled up the steep slopes in the hope of reaching a spot where I would no longer know which way to go, and just for that reason I would feel terror. But in vain; wherever I was I knew infallibly where I was; even without looking I could see the path that would lead me down again into the drowned valley. In the end I gave up the idea of getting lost. I turned downhill, and then, suddenly, I pushed myself down the frozen slope as one pushes a car to make the engine start. As I rushed downhill I screamed "Help! Help!" striving to hear the soft footstep of the pursuer. Then, just as suddenly, angry and ashamed, I stopped and laughed at the frozen forest. I made my way at my usual pace toward the mountaineers' hostel and saw Djurdja at the door, calling me.

Had I then known better how to read the signs I would have recognized in that laughter the first thawing of chill, of the giant glacier on which I had long been living like a penguin. Slowly, slowly, my Antarctic of dread began to thaw, the firm foothold drained away under my feet, the waters rose. The lack of fear which tormented me was really fear, its back turned to me; the floodwaters hardened into solid earth, to deceive the nonswimmers. What perfidy!

I screamed out, only many years later. In dream—though I never saw anything so concrete in reality—I saw that Burglar who wanted to sneak in through a glass panel in the door, by a secret, indirect route, as any repressed force does. I stopped him at the last moment though, to tell the truth, with outside help—they had awakened me and for a long time, or so it seemed, had been shaking me. The water had reached my throat and in that last tigerlike spring leaped up to quench the fading gleam of consciousness. That convulsive swaying of consciousness was the fear that nothing from the outside world could provoke—my blessing on all the flesh-and-blood burglars, on the air-raid sirens that howled over Zagreb like the hyaenas of war. All that seemed childishly innocent compared to that fear which came from within. Once that gleam has been crushed, we no longer know untroubled sleep. There is no more midnight Mirogoj, no provocation in the realms of Polypheme. For he whom I impersonated as a mockingbird, throwing pebbles into his mouth, stole up unheeded behind my back and rolled the stone to the opening of the cave.

Two or three years later, he broke in again. This time he didn't move, but stood in the room, a Faceless One, a terrifying Presence. The tocsin sounded within me, all the alarms, all the gadgets built into the gates of my temenos, all went into action and awoke me in time. This second time was more fearful than the first, for I had come to understand that he had obviously resolved not to break his ties with me. I asked myself, deranged: "Who is that? What is that?" blindly trying to associate him with some specific person in my life, with some specific conflict. But *who* was not the presentiment of evil, the stroke of the hour of the owl? *When* was there no conflict?

No, he was not anyone, he was not anything from without. He came from the primeval sludge, from the depths of self. He was the tail of the scorpion poised over its own spine, yearning for the suicidal spur. He was I, turned back upon myself.

He appeared a third time, too, though he did not show himself to me. In my bedroom above the Nile he tried to unravel the moonlit marquisette curtains. Not even the breathing of the child beside me deterred him. For all that, he was hampered before he was able to unravel the curtains. Frustrated. But he will come back. He will come back.

What kind of generators charge him? Obviously he is a suppressed part of my being, weighed down by his own undischarged energy, trying to break in where he could not enter normally. He is a medicinal draught, gulped with all its poisonous properties. The defect that made him possible must have so grown into me that it was invisible. It was

51

under my tongue, it was in the bright weave of my burdens, perhaps also in the very *sonde* with which I had sought to plumb my own depths. Certainly, the most difficult thing of all is to penetrate into one's own experience, and of all experiences the most difficult are those that cost us our lives.

But, as our bodies, those wise entities, have a marvelous defensive mechanism, a fantastic strategy, which has no equal even among the most perfect defensive systems that man has ever devised—the investigators of the body never cease to admire its inexhaustible conscious electronics—so also, only tenfold more dramatically, our pysche knows how to repel the onslaught of its enemies. Attacked by illness, it develops the capacity to heal itself. But we, unaccustomed to following events on that battlefield, don't see and don't know the wonders of that subtle duel. If we lend our ear to it we shall remain astounded, humbled, frightened, at the merciless dragons for which we are the battlefield.

Reason can throw no light on that treacherous twilight zone. Only foreboding and intuition which penetrate from below—or, rather, from above—turn our thoughts toward salvation, only they maneuver in a sea of living rocks, in jaws with antediluvian fangs. I don't understand but intuition tells me to doubt what would be the last thing to doubt: the Savior.

On those three occasions did I not catch a glimpse of his other face, that face which reveals itself when approached from the obverse side: is it possible that He who had followed me from my childhood wanted to drag me off three times to hell? Is it possible that it was the *animus mundi* that appeared, displaying his dark side to me?

That question shook me to the core. But once broached it could not be stopped, even as an earthquake cannot be stopped. Hastily, I asked myself another question: "And which is the reverse side one sees as Iblis?" And I replied at once, like a pupil who has long been waiting to be called: "The reverse side: isn't that to keep seeing and hearing him

52

exclusively, him the hidden one? To have the illusion that you hear his flute where there are only human voices?"

> You embraced me with God knows whose arms
> And kissed me with countless lips. . . .

and

> As in a covered Venetian gondola
> You waited for me in another's breath. . . .

Aren't those "God knows whose arms" and those "countless lips" now avenging themselves? Isn't it a revenge by that so-called heartless one, Theseus; isn't this his punishment meted to Ariadne? Gazing into the distance, didn't I fanatically ignore those near to me and thereby become changed into a destructive force which will in the end break into my spirit? To await the Right Moment prepare yourself for It and know not that the Right Moment is now; isn't it to be hungry and thirsty, gathering crumbs from the banquet at which I am the honored guest? A nearness unnoticed, a nearness overlooked, a nearness thrust aside—is that Frankenstein's monster, that murky apparition that doesn't give up, from which I fly and in my flight drive it to frenzy?

It is hard to delve deeper into the ditch of this question, down the axis of Janus's heads. It is hard to recognize beneath the mother's smile the merciless grimace of Kali. It is hard to recognize hatred in love. It is hard to doubt the light that leads you, to think that it turns on you by circuitous routes and pounces on you from behind, like shaggy darkness. I know that the last thing that I shall let slip is its silken train lined with scales of darkness. It is hard, finally, not to doubt even your own doubt; not to ask whose weapons are those: God's or the devil's?

But one must hope for something, even from oneself. I return to the foreboding that my own threatened psyche will find the remedy for itself. Don't the powers of destruction and the powers of integration flow parallel? Doesn't my very writing reveal a centripetal process, the chronicle of a soul that struggles gamely to arrange itself in the powers of a *yantra,* in a diagram of inner concentration? If the dividing line establishes itself in the shape of a *saoshyant* threatening to set free the beast within it, then it must struggle with the forces of healing that untiringly seek to heal its bisected shape. Desperate is that battle between two contesting yet inseparable forces, between Set and Horus, Ahriman and Ormuzd, The Prince and the Dragon (Baš-Čelik). Never has reason reached that battlefield; only the birds of my intuition fly to and fro uninterruptedly, bringing in their beaks *elixir vitae,* that draught which the apothecaries of the Middle Ages sought, that *succus lunariae* by which Isis restored the dismembered Osiris.

Or is that doubt in *Vox Dei* a skillfully thrown grenade of my demon? Is his cunning greater than my discernment? Is my talent to conceal myself greater than my ability to reveal myself?

Something speaks to me, something is silent.

OF SILENCE, IN WORDS

Behind the hills breathes the dragon of silence.
Over us fall the embers and the soot of that breath,
which is the word.

In a dangerous proximity, in the vicinity of silence, the word kept me company. I don't remember when I first sensed that it flinched as if scourged. It was the retreat of a guide who leads a traveler to the frontier of his kingdom and says to him: "We have reached the end of the world. Here begins that wilderness, that no man's land where my power ends." A proud advance was expected, an endless kingdom awaited, beyond which there were no more beginnings.

Therefore I don't know when I first felt the contact of Nothing, there where earlier the word used to touch me and with its touch convince me of Something. I think it was while I was still in Zagreb; I think it was when I was just beginning to write, but that was so long ago that I can no longer recall when it was. Maybe it never happened, maybe it was only a flash, yet this moment of awakening now unfolds, backward, its tiny uncertain story. No matter.

More certain than that is that Nothing can be touched, and that as much as Something, it is real to the touch. Even more, that on the other side of Nothing there are degrees of Nothingness; that the laws of its existence are tangible and that its qualities and conditions are comprehensible, and that the peculiarities of its Nothingness are exceptional. But, to be in contact with Nothing, a greater composure and patience was needed than I had at that unverified beginning.

Yes, it is possible strongly, very strongly, not to exist, or quite feebly.

It was, perhaps, only recently, on the balcony under the red lantern; quite recently at the bedside of a sick child; even more recently at a bus stop. Yet perhaps it was a long time ago, as I thought only a short while ago, without much confidence. But was it? So recently? So long ago?

The poem forced into retreat, plunged back into my throat, heavy and dead as graveyard soil. We began to talk about it on the first day and at once reached that frontier poem which cancels itself and devours into speechlessness the territories of speech and all its hopes. It thus happened that I knew nothing more, could do nothing more, felt nothing more. An immense deafness, an immense helplessness, ruled over me.

Then slowly, imperceptibly, in that immense deaf-and-dumbness of things I began to sense Nothing. I gazed around me, upward and downward, in front of me and behind me; I realized that the antiworld had absorbed me through one of its distant pores. I saw how from the far side of that divided countenance there quivered a turquoise breeze flecked with gold—it quivered like a bird which plummets to the depths of a mirror. Afterward I saw the place where only a short while before I had been the mother of two children; it recalled a flight emptied of birds. And I saw that all the treasures of that unworld were now mine. In return they sought only one of my surplus selves, only that one which takes form through words. On the farther side of the mirror was a whisper: They want you to renounce all that is most human in yourself: speech. O, gloomy words, how I loved you at that moment! In the hour of leave-taking, in the hour when you "returned work unfinished," abusing me through the first mouth that came my way.

Nothingness at first gave neither pain nor pleasure. Then slowly, imperceptibly, my unaccustomed senses began to grope with the colors of darkness. In that inner speechlessness there were stammerings of many silences, rasping and brilliant, never stilled, full as a well, stinging the blood like words. From the other side of the mirror the years when I hadn't written gave answer—when in all sorts of ways, when weak, when exuberant, when bloodless, when at full speed, I didn't write.

No, without regard for my many empty silences and the fact that my silence was often unintelligible and clouded, they were nevertheless wise years, wise as shame, wise as the most wise word that stumbles when uttering lies and nonsense. Thus, into the jaws of the great emperor of silence I threw without regret my virgin daughters, leaving them to his mercy, poem after poem. In return he rewarded me with all that I couldn't replant in the garden of speech.

That agreement with the dragon was probably only just concluded; but its fulfillment stemmed in effect from far earlier days. From a long time past. Long, long ago, perhaps even before that, even the least ambitious of my friends used to say: "Writing is work like any other. The risk involved is similar to any other. You may lose your grip. Your pen may rust. Your hand may stiffen. You must go on breaking the ice. You must live with rigor." I stayed silent, without understanding. When I was at my weakest I took pencil and paper, hoping that the others had been right. But everything ended with a bitter taste, in the pool of half-wits, the half-baked, the freaks. As soon as I felt somewhat stronger, I kept silent. A far-off time; a time of instinct and of not understanding. Then one denied without faith, without devotion; one didn't know that nonwriting is an active process, that silence is not simply a mere negation of speech but a strong inner counterargument—speech is a countercharged medium. Silence: fire and sulphur. Oh, more than that: the grave with presentiment of resurrection.

So were those years, which perhaps were not, which perhaps only are. Such is the moment which thinks that it cannot exist without predecessors. It revealed itself to me when I had sown that bread which I had been eating for years: recently. Not that it matters.

Look, I am no longer silent. I speak. I write as never before. My withdrawal is over, the term of the agreement has lapsed. That far-off, troubled, turbid period lasted until recently, that time in which only future words could prove that I existed before them. Even more, that I had kept silent because of them. Even more, that I was silent in their hearing.

I write in haste, feverishly, not correcting, not amending. I write with a child in my lap, with conversation on my lips. I make notes on a bus ticket, on the margin of a newspaper, on a towel. I continue in dream, I don't break off even when I walk. To think that I had once let slip every chance and a great deal of time; I no longer need time or chance. Words, so many words; they seek the lips like kisses after a long separation.

I keep silent, I am speechless at the opposite end of the coil, seeing that it is the goal of the other kingdom, an omen of the cradle.

"Objectively speaking," "working conditions" have never been so nonexistent for me as now, never have things and daily routines distracted me more, and never have I been less aware of them, that is to say never have I felt them more passionately. Can that have been "work"? I was working before, when I kept silent.

So many words. They seek the lips like kisses after a long separation. Like kisses that, perhaps, announce another, a final, separation.

ALEXANDRIAN TERZETTO

SOPRANO

In childhood the sound of words fascinated us; we didn't ask their meaning. The sound was enough for us. An unknown word would touch us with the feeler of its voice and lead us on through an impassable world; it was alive. When we came to know its "meaning" the word suddenly stopped, frozen as if by some evil spell; it became numbed. Why did we, Elizabeth, ever ask the surnames of our husbands?

I don't recall when 'alexandria' first struck my ear. Was it one of the pipes of the retired Dubrovnik sea captains that first puffed out the word, sailing under the walls of the gardens? Did it then infect the oleanders, the laurels, the cypresses, and all the rest of their woodland kin? Or was the pipe long superseded by my mother's aunt Emma, who used to pass her winters in "alexandria" and "cairo" and who pulled out yellowing photographs of balls *"an der schönen blauen Donau"*? I don't recall what images were puffed out from the old gentlemen's pipes—images puffed out like the south wind, like recollections. But I do recall most clearly the smoke from the pipes and the scent of the late-flowering magnolias and, most certainly, "alexandria." It was a sound interlined with the most real fantasy. Heavily orchestrated, it passed through hundreds of sounds—shells, sirens, throats not quite human. It had a vague connection with the sea and with bananas. It was something closer, more tangible, than gay Vienna. O alexandria, O you wonder! Where shall we once again meet?

But I remember very well the day when I first entered Alexandria. Not from Vienna but from Cairo, along a road which long, for very long, trickles through the desert and then nervously cuts through the Mareotis marshes. It was on that very day that alexandria definitely settled on the shores of the Mediterranean and became transformed into a marvelous, ancient, and ailing city. On that day I was deafened, exploring my one-time orchestra. Alexandria. Before its final soundless existence, that first inaudible sound, that smoke from the captains' pipes, that aroma of a powdered waltz, hovered about my head for the last confused time—like a bird about a fallen nest. O Alexandria, O you wonder! When shall we, where shall we, part?

CYMBALS

Courtesans and philosophers have always slept in the same quarters of the city. Thaïs of Ptolemy and Thaïs of Paphnutius, both woven into the tapestry of Cleopatra—the courtesan of history. But those who knew how to love, who knew how to hate, have died: her generals and merchants, her mathematicians and *bon vivants*, her sages, beggars, and saints, and her three-headed lover: Caesar-Antony-Octavian.

Alexandria is a coquette, generous and belonging to no man. Cairo yearns for her, as rough sheiks yearn for white-skinned, blue-eyed foreigners from the north. They disembark there, dusty and full of longing, thirsty for blueness and whiteness, eager for that incomparably good-humored voluptuousness that reveals her mystery.

Wherever you may happen to be in Alexandria you sense the sea—its aroma, its moisture, its sound, and the steep flight of the city toward the burning sands. There are profoundly similar cities tied to that power of water—cities such as Benares. Both Alexandria and Benares rush downward to the water like the eager mouths of a countless herd. One sunny December morning, before seven o'clock, I was wandering in Benares, in its unraveled maze of tiny alleys which grow thin like capillaries in a single leprous and sacred flesh. And each one of those capillaries led me circuitously to the Ganges.

Alexandria is much simpler; its streets, drawn by a Euclidean ruler, rush precipitously toward the sea, not concealing their desire, eager for enjoyment. And all those streets, all those straight yet supple outlines lose their mood in the sinuous shore, in a curve that follows the line of the waves. The convolutions of the brain splashed by primeval vision, the convolution in touch with primeval matter, washes upon it—that is the Alexandrian coastline, seen from the land, seen from the sea, seen from the air.

This spotless view of the sky is still full of scars from radiant, flaming gnostic thought. Here it was that Greek thought broke loose from the moorings of Aristotelian dogma and ventured out to meet the ocean, caring naught for its inability to swim. Alexandria has never been an Egyptian city; it was a Greek city ennobled by the mystery of Egypt; a city that nurtured equally tenderly Plotinus and Euclid, Mark and Thrasyllus, Clement and Eratosthenes, Augustine as well as Heron.

Here the Corpus Hermeticum was codified and translated; here the first maps of the world were outlined; catalogues of writers and books were compiled, editions of Homer and translations of the Old Testament were ordered. The Museum and the Library were the focus and the crossroads of Greek and Middle East savants; they came from Samos, from Cyrene, from Aeolia, from Ephesus, from Petra, from Sicily, from Tyre. Here was drawn up the principle of three-dimensional space from which we haven't emerged for twenty centuries. Here the earth spun about the sun and became a sphere. Here the fireworks of Heron hissed. Here was gathered, pedantically, every sort of knowledge, piled up in rows, on shelves, in files. Alexandria had everything, permitted everything: academies and taverns, shameless booths and fanatic hermits, alchemic retorts and flowing amphoras.

How easy it is to recall all that, on some balcony, in some sticky casino, no matter where. As easy as it is difficult to bring to life Babylon or Amarna, Byblos or Mohenjo-Daro. In those places the landscape is exhausted and gives no picture of life long ago. But the landscape of Alexandria is inexhaustible, so created that a life of deep abundance, foaming a little on the surface, lives forever.

Alexandria exhales a mood of sullen melancholy. Those who have created it over so many long years are leaving: Greeks, Jews, Italians, French, Armenians, Turks, English, all are moving away. Everything is rusting and disintegrating; the Greek taverns, the unpredictable little cafés, the restaurants à la Trianon or Athens, the exclusive yacht clubs, the Jesuit colleges, the carnivals, all are slowly and sadly disappearing. It is sad to meet in the side streets some elderly couple, a little shabby, walking slowly and carefully on tottering feet, worn out, extenuated, enveloped in a cloud of quiet conversation in Greek or in any of the aging languages of Alexandria.

With the grief of the oppressed, depart those who fostered the famous qualities of Alexandria: its quick-wittedness, its perversity, its scandals, its repentance, its wealth. Behind the ailing beauty lies the viscid, glutinous stagnant water where clouds of mosquitoes rise. The thick green cataract of old age impairs the sight of the Cyprus doves.

Blue-eyed, golden-haired, and white, white . . . Aphrodite, censed with Sabaean incense, with Egyptian cosmetics on her dark eyes . . . Thaïs, Cleopatra, Thaïs . . . the eternally prodigal who sleep in the same quarters as the sages.

GONG
Strolling along the esplanade of Alexandria for the nth time,

I realized that there was no help for me, for I knew that I could only be in one place at one time: nowhere. Where is Alexandria now? In vain I touch its stone, its wind, its sea; it is as if I were touching some star in an astronomical atlas, as if I were drinking water from a pictured well.

Turning despairingly from all this thankless geography, I begin revengefully to summon words, words, words. Sentences which I will pour out on paper buzz through my head. Alexandria would then be a butterfly upon a pin; the mummy of a summer, but mine.

Thus, in a house of syllables, we meet for the third time. Outside, the angry multitude roars; outside, the furies rage. A sweet shudder shakes the shattered bricks, as if announcing a leave-taking. Love, nothing can be possessed, either in the hand or on paper; only in the heart. Alexandria, so much are you mine, so much I love you. O never sufficiently mine, stone cast into an abyss.

ONE NIGHT IN THE WORLD

*One of my eyes is blind, the other has second sight;
they travel with the same tears through the night
of the world.*

One night, in Alexandria, bathing in the stilled sea, I saw the visible part of death; it gleamed dully on the distant horizon, like oxidized aluminum. Neither sky nor sea, an indeterminate nirvana. From that space without contours, without movement, something called, its mouth pursed as if drinking through a straw, like nostrils bent over still unsmoldering incense.

Up till that night I had been without any true picture of death: not in the sound of the raven, or in the living hair of dead Mario, was I able to recognize death with any certainty. Least of all in the banal trappings of the funeral ritual. Perhaps it was the fullness of life that most recalled death to me: the golden sheen of summer noons, the pomegranate bursting under the pressure of its own fruitfulness.*
But in the sea stretched out like a turbid dark-gray fabric on which feet raise clouds of sandy dust, the depth of that

---

* The more beautiful, the more swollen the pomegranate, the more death-summoning. The scent of its fall is most intense on the heights. On petty heights we don't feel the magnetism of depth. It blooms only in space and distance. The flower casts its seed far from the calyx, like the words of a prophet far from his homeland.

horizon without outlines, without points of reference, without surface, that pure formlessness alone that hems the world in which I squirm, there at last was the true face of death.

Into that nothingness you go alone—under your skin there's room only for you. The waters close in a ring about you, about your flanks, then about your waist, and then about your throat. The sand, gently and irresistibly, gives way beneath your feet until they begin to flutter above it, rise from walking to hovering and your whole body is freed from its weight and the leaden support of the sea bed, like the weed it finds along its pliant way.

Seen by day, it is the usual landscape. It begins at the tiny island where every morning an unskilled military volley hunts the mad little plane which loops the loop and plunges toward the open sea. Everything is so reassuring, so normal, to the left of the island; there is preparation for war; the machine guns are loaded, the mines are tested. But at night that so ordinary a sight turns its entrails inside out, betrays itself as a terrifying, mighty formlessness and we appear as a nourishing fluid by which it is always being filled and yet always remains unfilled.

One night in Gwalior I felt that my life was indestructible. I sang as I walked down that steep, stony ridge, on whose summit rose the wonderful palace of Man-Mandir. The taut crest of the hill and the outline of the fortress, which slashed like a dagger into the night riddled with stars, and even the man walking beside me, lighting my way with a lantern, everything was carved out of the most profound silence, from its hardest and deepest layer. My voice took nothing from it, added nothing to it; my voice was breadth in a world wherein Gwalior was height. See how my voice and this silence make this expanse possible, through separation; and when one day height lies upon breadth, time will stop and we shall flatten it between ourselves like a leaf of the finest gold.

I went down by one of the gates of the Gwalior island, where a cab was waiting to take me to the railway station; from that station I would travel in a sooty train along the plain eastward to a little town which is not even marked on the map, where a ramshackle bus would take me to the temples at Kadjuraho. This journey through India was a unique spectacle of separation from what is most beautiful. Every little place, every temple, every meeting, became that one and only finally discovered landscape of my soul; every time I took leave of my whole self, yet every time I would re-emerge as soon as I turned my back on it. It is thus that indestructible life travels; renewing itself by contact with every loss.

As my body went down, my heart rose. Below, in the obscurity of the plain, but without fear, with confidence that I would return and ascend once more to the colossal fortress, I would go up again by that same steep path, under the same stars and with the same invulnerable silence around my own voice. Coming down, I shouted: "Till we meet again! Till we meet again!" until I no longer knew what was echo and what a living voice.

THE STARS RUSH, CLAIRVOYANT, BLINDLY
OUR EYES FOLLOW THEM

Last night, on the balcony of a summer villa in Mamurra, this verse burst out of a long-sunken layer of my consciousness. Ten years earlier it was, roughly speaking, on the surface. Probably the sight of the night sky touched some numbed nerve in which still flowed the last tremors of an exhausted sensation.* This evening that verse sounds powerless and poignant, reminding me of a child that shakes its fist against the thunder. But when I lean over my well and listen intently I still hear the fading echo of that verse and see the scope of its illumination in the night around me.

The stars rush blindly, our clairvoyant eyes follow them. That verse says that man's vision is the cosmos and all else is chaos. That verse says that our very perception of the blind onrush sows in it harmony and purpose. So I believed at that time, so I wanted to believe. In that lay my defensive perspectives, my trenches and my ramparts. I feared the incalculable depths of the heavens and defied my own insignificance by "adding" something of myself to the world; vainly I contributed to its creation, peering through my

---

* Perhaps that is not really so. My spiritual Atlantis is perhaps very much alive; perhaps its workshops mass-produce its goods, full steam ahead, not caring if those above demand them or not. Like an atomic calendar that, once wound up, turns its gearwheels in a world in which time is no longer of value.

loopholes into the chaotic gloom, reciting incantations against fear.

Naturally, in the depths of my soul, I knew that truth was in fact the opposite. Reality—and not I—was the more perfect cosmic teammate. I was the blind, unsettled, scattered pole of that dynamic field. Not only was I unable to contribute but I was not even able to create. The most that, then and now, I could do was: recognize it.* The effort of creation, isn't that the effort to come closer to that which is more perfect than we are? To higher awareness of the stars, let's say.

Today I rewrite that almost forgotten verse, so that in it I give the stars their proper place:

> The stars rush, clairvoyant,
> Blindly our eyes follow them. . . .

---

* We go into the world and recognize it. What? The fragments of a huge body, the dismembered Osiris. Infinitesimal indications of a Presence. Through our recognition, through our memory, we give back its image to that scattered reality, its wholeness, what it is and what we are.

OF THE SAME MATTER WHICH FORMS THE SEA MUST ALSO BE MY THOUGHT OF THE SEA. . . .

I don't know how many times I had to go to the shores of the Mediterranean to feel the longing to write a poem that would be "sea," with its sounds and its surges and its murmurs. I know that I don't like "murmurs" in poetry. I would say that I had passed by the temptations of Sound, as past harmless Sirens, a little put out that they were so lacking in allure. But there, on the southern shore of the great Blue Goddess, on the dazzling white sand as fine as flour, with waves never still for three hundred and sixty days in the year . . . there, before the great emerald melting into the still greater turquoise . . . there I strove to give my words the substance of that murmur and that foam, not to speak but to murmur.

> From far away we speak to the sea,
> From far away the sea speaks to us:
> "Murmuring, everything is only a murmur
> And the words that you hear are only
> The strain of distance which binds
> Both murmurs into a knot, the knot of speech.
> Tirelessly it summons us in a voice
> Which in its nearness is not heard."

Somewhere on the beach, I declaimed that poem, aloud, resolutely, as words that must be impressed upon my listener while they were still warm. And my listener was someone who was not present, someone who knew how to demand in a serious voice, as if he were himself the Little Prince: "Tell me something like the sea." As I spoke, I heard it and the sea grew calm.

I hurried to my deck chair which all morning had been falling into the treacherous sand, like a monument. I wrote down "something like the sea" to see how it looked on paper. On paper it rasped like a sick man and then was quiet. "Tell me something like the sea." I heard that serious boy once more. And the sea, that enormous turquoise that flowed into the still-greater emerald, once again announced itself with all its force.

For the sea lives in another house and our words about the sea in yet another. My inadvertent listener on the shore felt most painfully that dissolution. With one hand he gripped the sea and with the other the poem, striving to tie them in a knot. Since he could not—since he could not even let each go its own way—he tried to reconcile them in a final and violent manner.

I don't know how many times I had to come to the shores of the Mediterranean to hear the voice of my dead comrade, a voice that could not be heard from nearby.

PROFILE OF A QUEEN

*You travel among the living and they don't suspect
it; they sit and are silent, gazing at something that
you alone see.*

One September evening, on the beach at Mamurra, I saw
the profile of Queen Ahmet on the body of a very ordinary
bather. The same enigmatic lips that mark the beginning—
or the end—of a smile, the same gently curved nose that
continually breathes in something deep and passionate. All
the scents of Egypt caress those nostrils and the breast
proudly swells like the sail of a felucca filled to the gunwale
with narcotic incense which no other nose is able to recognize.

That face lives only for itself: the enigmatic beginning-
end of that smile knows that that small cuckoo brain which
has made its nest in the noble skull is really only a guest in
something immeasurably wiser than itself. The woman murmurs like a huge, fat cat. She purrs something to her drowsy
husband, who does not listen with enjoyment, floundering
in the hot fine sand. I look, entranced, at her absorbed profile; I watch how her lips, wise and wonderful petals, let
those chirping, twittering intruders pass. The profile lets
them coo, lets them play, allows passage through the throat,
while the profile itself, free and aloof, reveals ancient Sabean
thoughts in its enigmatic features. It inhales all that summer

landscape, the turquoise rose of the sea; it drinks up the brilliance that gilds the dust of its graveyard. . . . O Ahmet! Whence have you been sent and who sent you to our world? And what is that secret aim you have within you?

Four thousand times has the earth circled around the sun since men saw for the first time you whom the sun god visited, so that Hatshepsut, "the most beautiful among the beautiful," should conceive. Perhaps that was not the first time. Perhaps you visited men from the depths of some long-sunken civilization which had learned the secret of time travel.

The wind blew out of the red eye of the sun and the bathers began to move away like drifting dandelion seed. When I lowered my gaze from the open sea to the now chill sand, the queen's profile had already withered, drifting away like perfume down some evening-scented garden.

STROLLING THROUGH THE CAIRO MUSEUM

I am that part of my dream which is nightmare; my hands, my feet, my mind, and my conscience are that part of my soul into which has been banished its malady and its death.

INTRODUCTION

Museums are places of execution. In them die ingloriously those faint sparks of curiosity that light up within us when we first come face to face with unknown cities, races, inheritances. We enter the doors of museums like untrained soldiers; and within, there awaits us an army of thirty centuries. Magnetisms bombard us from all sides, murderous orgies drink us, a great dream raises its monster head, swallower of small, short-lived dreamers. A bodiless multitude pours out from the corners and chokes us, slowly and gleefully, until at last, indifferent and truly strangled, we rush head over heels through the remaining seventy halls, past seventy-seven showcases, seeing nothing—corpses on living legs.

I have dragged myself, wearily, through the museums of Europe; I have emerged, shattered, from the museums of Athens, Zurich, Naples, Paris, and Baghdad, swearing that never again would I pit myself against such voracious organisms. Like a mist I grew translucent in the concentrated brilliance of the Louvre and the Vatican, evaporated in the galleries of Florence and Venice. But in India, in that unintended museum, which allows for pauses amid powerful experiences—that living museum, untouched by guards—I traveled, strengthening in myself my ability for absorption.

After a three-year pause I again found myself faced by a mammoth storehouse of energy, before one of the greatest of its kind—the Cairo museum.

BUDDHA AND OSIRIS

Each of these figures is a world entire, which doesn't suffer anything but itself. From each of them one can only advance by descending, for each is the fruit of supreme maturity.

No smile glitters on the lips of the Egyptian statues as it glitters on the lips of the Indian idols. Even when they are portraits—and they are usually portraits—the faces are unbending, physically deathless. They are a part of the tangled equations of the body, a part of calculations that do not reveal motion, gaze, or quiver of the lips, but only a magical mathematics, sister of the sacred Tibetan geometry—the *yantra*.

On the lips of the Mahavira trembles a smile more enigmatic than any that has posed the riddle of the Gioconda —an arhat smile, turned inward, bliss without the blissful one, a journey without a traveler.

The faces of Egyptian kings, priests, scribes, nobles are faces of men long dead. Life has moved elsewhere—into a formula, into a magic number, in harmony with the canon laid down by the priests and followed by the artists. The faces are there that they may be recognized by the ka, that double which hovers around them like a bird around a deserted nest. For this art is devoted to death and its aims. These statues are intentionally emptied of life, intentionally transformed into vessels, into garments, which life will again fill when the time is ripe.

On one of my strolls through these soul-snatching corridors of statues I was astounded by the face of Osiris, the face of Him into Whom after Death Every Man Is Transformed. A very sharp and noticeable frontier is drawn between the faces of men and the faces of gods. The face of Kefren is the face of Kefren. Thothmes is Thothmes and no one else, the face of So-and-so is the face of So-and-so. But the face of Osiris is the *face of the soul*. The features of all men are there—welded, merged with his. Osiris's face is no man's face; it is a *state of mind*. In that, he reminds me of the Buddha and his indescribable, inscrutable smile. Every other ancient Egyptian face insists on regular, indivisible features, for how otherwise could his ka recognize him? But Osiris is what he is, above the individual atman, the life principle. I stand astounded on that clear and definite frontier which the ancient Egyptian artist crossed with such sobriety and ease, as if he himself had experienced all the levels of existence before he modeled them.

HATSHEPSUT

The face of Hatshepsut—to which so many vigorous and masculine traits have been attributed—is as if carved of cotton and not of rose-colored granite. The face is soft and melts under one's gaze. I am unable to recall its lines. For those lines are bashful and slip across the face as uneasy shadows slip across the sky. She is large, feline, womanly, melancholy, Hatshepsut, "first among the loveliest."

Even when it is on the body of the Sphinx, that face is in no way expressive. And when the Pharaonic beard encircles it, when a sacrifice is to be made, it is as fluid as water. Nonetheless, that woman sent an important mission to a distant, still-unidentified, land of the South; she ruled despite the anger and hatred of her relatives and her court, despite the love—perhaps—of her favorite, despite the fact that she was a woman, the "first among the loveliest."

Her hardness and her strength the sculptor has concealed somewhere outside her—in the heart of the ibis which flies in the body of the falcon which flies in the eye of Horus. In such heights burns out her secret.

Her cheeks are oval, dreamy. A huge cotton hill carved in the body of a lioness, on a plinth of the hardest Egyptian stone: Hatshepsut, hidden heroism.

EYE OF THE CLAIRVOYANT PHARAOH

In that inexhaustible museum, in the hall of Akhenaten, there is a portrait of a woman absorbed in thought, the Queen Nefertiti, Nefer-i-iti (the beautiful one has come), without diadem and without jewelry. The new wave of Egyptologists and aesthetes cry: "You are even more beautiful than you were in your youth! More spiritual!" But except for this head there is nothing of greater or different beauty save its famous rival, the Swanlike She Herself who now languishes in the Berlin Museum, a kidnapped princess. It is a summons to follow the ways and metamorphoses of the face that turned away from the faith of its time, the face that wished to penetrate into the inner splendor of the sun's disk.

That first face, the celebrated stolen head, sways on its long neck in an aureole of mild and pure spirit. In that face is summarized all that is fragile and touching, a charm that exists only in a world of disproportionately thin stems and much too heavy flowers. That was the beauty that pleased the soul of the moody Pharaoh, a flower illuminated by the inner splendor of the sun.

The second portrait seems to have been carved some years later than the first, though we have no reliable proof of that. Both were found at Amarna, in the workshop of the master sculptor. Each seems made of a different substance, the first face of flowers and of dreams, the second of awakening and ripeness. In those few hypothetical years that separate one portrait from the other, Egypt had compressed the experience of a whole century. The undercurrent that had advanced from the time of the first dynasties leaped of a sudden into the sun, spurred on by the furious temper of Akhenaten's will. Was Akhenaten a tumor on the brain of the

Egyptian giant? Was he a clairvoyant sickness of civilization? If he was, then Nefertiti was his most wakeful, most clairvoyant eye.

The portrait found in the workshop of the master sculptor Thutmosis is unfinished. The queen lacks the royal diadem, her face is incomplete. Therefore her features appear simpler and purer than those of the young Nefertiti. This is no longer the swan in its aureole of sad eyes, this is no longer the great fragile flower ready to tremble in the winds of history. This face is now its own wind, its own trembling. Raised gently, as if devoted to an immense silence, with traces of fatigue because of the voices that disturb its peace.

Beautiful one, what have you seen behind the sun's disk? Still lighter light or still darker dark? She reveals to no one what she has seen; she goes on drinking up more and more avidly some sight we cannot see. She doesn't see it with her eyes, she sees it with all her incomparably lovely features, she gazes at it with a movement of her neck. Like some great ear she bends her head to the silence that can be heard in the heavens; the head of a nun, of a medieval *yogina*, of a Buddhist *thera*. She is stripped of that beauty that can be stripped; transformed into an inner brilliance of the sun, in a likeness that has been imbued with the most sensitive gaze of that time; impaled on the point of that gaze, all brought into bloom in her pupils, which widen before the final vision.

Nefertiti, the aging queen, the great eye with which the clairvoyant Pharaoh gazes into the invisible.

THE FALCON
High above me, black and powerful, whirls the huge falcon, "its right eye the sun and its left the moon." The sound is like the boom of a world gong. I am unable to paint in words that dark granite and the terrible power of those folded wings. It is a target to aim at, the flight of all flights. He and I, we are the targets to hit Ourselves.

We have read so much in books about the falcon, that falcon; how often we have looked at it, black and white on paper, but here, eye to eye with it, it leaves us stricken under its talons, powerless and dead. We are not things, we are those who are dead, we are small motionless specks in the flowing diamond of the cosmos, and around us are living granite falcons, created from hardened black consciousness. How evanescent is my body, made from what coarse essence! Yet through it sieves the fine, thick magnetism of the black falcon, passing through it as water through sand. I feel it as it passes, I feel that I am letting it through. I feel that I am losing something inestimably divine and strong. But I am so made that I must lose it.

Farewell, black falcon. I must come to you with a different body, later, after a hundred years, so, till we meet again—perhaps.

THE DISMEMBERED OSIRIS

What does the dismembered Osiris dream, if indeed he dreams at all? His seventy-two pieces are scattered on the land; each of them dreams its dream of reassembling and resurrection, each suffers because of its displacement. But already over the earth is passing the great healer, Iset; that much-loved, scattered body draws her irresistibly; she collects it, recognizes it, and puts it together in a living whole. Under her hands, Osiris will rise from the dead.

In this myth is prefigured the destiny of our soul. Our soul is the lost part, our soul is the divine whole. Our soul dreams its vision of reuniting and rising from the dead, our soul awakens in a whole Self.

We are all the dismembered God; and the power of healing is never far away, that power which has already healed us countless times and which will, in every new Kalpa, heal us once more.

The highest categories are inexpressible in the language of psychology, in the language of philosophy, in the language of physics; only shyly do myth and poetry touch them.

THE BODY, A SEALED VASE

The body of the Egyptian queen, saint, goddess, is a sealed vase and above it a face guards the secret. It reminds us that all is within, firm, concealed from the eye of the uninitiated. To approach the body more closely we must draw nearer with a different sense of space and time within us. From ancient art we can take only as much as we believe that which it believed.

But who will convince us of that, we who have come filled with disbelief that anything ever existed before us?

Were we to break the seal on the vase in the vain search for its essence, the smoke that would rise from it would take the shape of the world, but only after our departure from that place. To touch that body in the space in which it lives means to understand that there is no "inner" even as there is no "outer," that everything is present everywhere, passionate and very dense, so passionate, so dense, that it cannot expand any more and touches the very rim of emptiness.

NUT

Until I saw in an Egyptian tomb our mother Nut, I had thought that the sun was the most powerful thing in the world.

Nut is Hathor is Uazit is Isis—is a starry sky, the world's cow, the winged cobra. All that is Isis, is Hathor, is Nut.

Nut is the deep blue of the universe, studded with golden stars. Raised above the male earth, she supports herself on feet and hands, and lightly, very lightly, sets limits to the beginning and the end of terra firma. The limbs of our mother Nut fall just as the smoke rises upward, bodiless, swaying and tender.

Nut is Hathor is Uazit is Isis. At the close of each day she devours her own child, the blazing sun. Swallowed, the sun travels by night through her dark-blue body till, in the morning, it is born just as a woman gives birth. The blazing sun travels under her maiden womb and at night returns to its mother through her lips.

79

Until I had seen our mother Nut I had thought that the sun was the most powerful thing on earth. But one dark Theban fresco shows that she awaits it every day, every eon, to swallow it and to guide it through her own body, through the entrails of the world; for the millionth time Nut, the voracious Madonna, the *mater virgo*, the deep maidenhead of the skies, falls upon us as the sacrificial smoke rises upward.

THE VEILED ISIS
A being who in the palm of one hand holds the viscous germ from which one is born and in the other, equally tenderly, the dust of one's bones . . . and then shifts them from palm to palm, as if in play, now faster, now slower . . . till they are completely mingled and it is no longer known what each hand holds . . .

Her body is solidified time; all our existence is in it. Nor can she do without a single one of our silly little minutes.

Her face which is constantly revealed is present in all the parts of her body. But we have eyes only for her veil. Isis, thy nakedness is invisible to us.

He who sees you will never again see anything else. He who touches you will never again touch anything else. Long-forgotten priests from Philae and Bubastis, from On and Memphis, still have not taken their gaze from you. In Sais you appeared to the wondering Plutarch: "I am everything that was, everything that is, and everything that will be and no mortal has ever lifted my veil!"

You are time, Isis, only a point motionless in the universe. We are those who circle around you.

POEM BEFORE THE STATUE OF PTAH
All the six gates open in your gaze, only the seventh is closed; that one which gleams in the depths as at the bottom of a well. With a golden bee as its lock. Through them you pass, bent and small, so narrow and low are they that you

can enter only naked and alone . . . just as you come before the Supreme Presence. There will I pass bare to the bone; the golden bee will buzz and fly away and I will stride on into space beyond your gaze, into the space that I have so greatly implored.

Thus traveled the most ancient traveler in the subterranean lands, Innan, the lover of Dumuzi; before her terrible twin Ereshkigal she traveled because of her desire for kidnapped Dumuzi. Ishtar traveled there out of desire for Tammuz; thus the winged souls of the Egyptians traveled into the lands of King Osiris. So, too, traveled the Brahmin boy Nachiketa and Orpheus, his grandchild. There traveled our own Kosjenka, the inquisitive little fairy. And all of them returned, still stronger, still more immortal.

What is there behind those gates with the golden bee as keyhole? Your gaze is the passage that emerges at the surface of my eye. There, behind those gates with the golden bee as keyhole, *there am I!* Will they recognize me, will they recognize me? Better keep my eyes shut lest I be frightened by what my eyes light on. Better keep my ears blocked lest I am lured by something terrible, as a human cry. Better block my nose lest the lotus beguile me. Better beat into the dust my touch, make bellows of my skin and throw in a corpuscle of my blood and bear it to the nearest water.

Only then will I recognize myself—when there remains only what cannot be destroyed. And that is I.

BEAUTY AND THE BEAST

In the heart of the fire nestles a cold spot; no one knows any longer what is ember, what is ice.

It is clear why beauty seeks out the beast; it trusts only the beast. With it, it feels most intensely what it is—beauty. Nowhere is this shown in greater relief than in the lovely profile of the delicate Nefertiti against the background of those distorted features, in the fascination of that sickly, repulsive, deformed Pharaoh who described her in noble words, full of tenderness—which is even more repulsive—as the most beloved of all the rulers of the thirty Pharaonic dynasties.*

Great beauty is a great burden. Beautiful women are enslaved beings, endlessly dependent on all who desire them; they are extraordinarily able and shrewd at constantly stirring up that desire. In that tireless task, in some way panic-stricken, the great beauty begins not to notice who is beside her; she sees no one's face, she sees only, more cloudy or more clear, the mirror that convinces her that she is alive. Beauty does not live of itself, but from others; others indeed give their

---

* "Heiress, great blessing, lady of mercy and of sweet love, Mistress of South and North, beautiful of face, joyous between the sheets, favorite of the living Aten, first-crowned wife of the King who loves her, Our Lady of the Two Lands, she of great love, Nefertiti, who lives forever."

lives for her, but they do not live from her, they live from their own giving.

But it is not clear what the beast searches for in the embrace of the beauty, the bodily monstrosity in close contact with that perfectly pure and noble form. Didn't it feel still more ugly, didn't it feel that it was not in a state to possess that beauty, such loveliness unattainable under its hands?

Unless the beast assumes that the beauty needs it more than it needs the beauty, it cannot relax and calm down in a world in which the beauty's role is so creative. Was that the relationship of Akhenaten to Nefertiti, that unreal fragile little girl who was perhaps of his own kin, perhaps an imported little princess from the kingdom of Mitanni, perhaps the daughter of some powerful local noble, but who became a queen without whose name and image not a single royal edict was issued?

As the years passed, her face with its ideally pure features came more and more to resemble Akhenaten's. Akhenaten and Nefertiti were the standard-bearers of a new faith, of a new freedom. That faith identified them in the artist's eyes. But that is not the whole answer. Pharaoh's ugliness became the fashion of the time; Pharaoh's repulsiveness—and not the beauty of his consort—Pharaoh's ugliness peeps out from all the faces in the short and violent epoch of Amarna.

In truth, men lived feverishly at Amarna in those days; they carved hurriedly, built hurriedly, sang, prayed, loved. For time was divorced from eternity and flowed in a dramatic, human torrent. It was a world of consciously disrupted laws. Caricatures peeped out on all sides. The grotesque lived in symbiosis with a strange Gothic elegance, with which the human face suddenly trembled. No one knew any more what was beautiful.

Looking at a clay tablet from Amarna, dug up in the workshop of the great Thuthmosis, it is difficult to differentiate Akhenaten's profile from Nefertiti's. The artist saw her as the splendor of ugliness; and so, too, he saw those five or six daughters of hers, and so in the end he saw everything he cast eyes on. Thuthmosis's workship is full of misplaced lines, like pictures in a distorting mirror. And it is actually from Thuthmosis's mirror that the spectacle of Amarna looks at us, divorced from all traditional checks and balances, a sight like those seen in hashish smoke or in the eyes of a gifted seer. It is the sight of a divine monster who devours all the beautiful women and handsome men of his kingdom. Why didn't it happen the other way around? Why didn't beauty prove itself more fascinating than ugliness?

It will be said: because the repulsiveness was Pharaoh's. And Pharaoh is, as is well known, the ka of all Egypt, the life-giving spirit of the land, the spirit that enables millions of Egyptians to exist, which supports its topocosmos, making possible within it a harmonious relationship between animals, harvests, and flood waters. Pharaoh is the incarnation of the supreme power and, as such, cannot be other than beautiful.

A good answer but, at best, incomplete. For what are we to say about those hundred or more Pharaohs who reigned before and after Akhenaten, and who left the world at peace and didn't impose their own image on it? Why was it just Akhenaten? That supernatural ugliness? And, having done that, why did he esteem his bodily aberrations more than the harmony of the being nearest to him?

Because he was a prophet, you will say. Because he forged the New Times; because he impressed the seal of his whole being on those New Times, created them in his own image. Because everything was consecrated to a religious and aesthetic dogma that he created through his own hallucinated prism. For him the state was too cramped to become identified with it; in truth, without the ruler's recalcitrance and with the piety of a mystic, he could shout out: "The Time; it is I!" Such an answer would almost satisfy us, were it not for the most recent archeological revelations at Karnak, which show, once and for all, that it was really the fragile Nefertiti who forged the New Times. Not only was she Pharaoh's inspiration, but also the real *spiritus movens* with whom the opponents of the Aten cult reckoned far more mercilessly than with Akhenaten himself.* But if, as it seems, Nefertiti was a prophetess, why didn't the new movement stand under the banner of her transcendent beauty?

The Amarna episode becomes more and more mysterious with every fresh revelation.

Neither before nor afterward in Egyptian civilization was the artist so liberated from the canons of sacred ritual geometry as in the times of short-lived Amarna. Never before or after was he free to search with so much embittered passion for the new field of displaced balance. To contemporaries, that art, which is so close to us, must have seemed unbearably anarchic; that art which exhaled the most systematic and most consistent thought of the Egyptian genius.

Akhenaten raised no objection to the artist portraying him as he was: by a caricature of face and body. He was too great a devotee of Maat—the man of truth—to have desired the idealization of his face. More than twenty colossal statues show him with obese flanks and a woman's stomach, with drawn and sickly face and distorted features. Behind this

* In recent years about forty thousand fragments of Nefertiti's and Akhenaten's palace at Tell-el-Amarna were found in a pylon at Karnak. The area of the northern royal palace was sufficient to enclose both Versailles and Fontainebleau. The rooms in the palace were painted with scenes from the Pharaoh's family life and with thanksgivings to Aten. The Pharaoh Horemheb, the later restorer of the ancient cult of Ammon, meticulously and mercilessly smashed to bits the countless frescoes and the statues of Akhenaten and Nefertiti, in order to make use of them later as building rubble to fill the entrails of the gigantic pylon at Karnak. The world of Amarna, Aten's world, was crumbled into ten thousand fragments and all those fragments piled together and carefully immured. But that was not enough for Horemheb. As the fragments were being piled up, he vengefully and sadistically hanged the queen—at least her picture—upside down, to degrade her memory even there, where no one would ever see it. He didn't deal with Akhenaten in this way. Didn't his unchivalrous behavior show who was the real champion of the Aten revolution?

chill, perverted mask, a spirit was imprisoned which wrote the most exalted and impassioned song of praise to the sun and which brought human tenderness and warmth to the stone reliefs and scenes of court life. From the carved stone radiates the devotion and enthusiasm of the man-ruler, not the god-ruler, his devotion to his god, his wife, his children. In every carved stone flickers the blessed rain of the sun's hands and human hands raised in greeting to this light, like pious flowers. Akhenaten was a poet who, as if by a coarse jest, found himself on the throne of a despot. Tell-el-Amarna was his true *asilum*, the enchanted refuge behind whose walls the kingdom suddenly disintegrated. They took from the Pharaoh's rule cities and the princedom of Syria; one by one his vassals fell away. Akhenaten's banished viceroy in Gebel, in his last despairing letter to his sovereign, wails prophetically not over lost Gebel but over Tell-el-Amarna itself: "O king my master, O king my master, save that city from shame. . . ."

A tremendous number of studies of Akhenaten's face exist. It fascinated the sculptors and they modeled it tirelessly, penetrated into it, intentionally distorted it, to madness, to malice, and then restored his original features, powerless before them. That face became the pictorial dogma of the times. It slowly disintegrated everything known until then; all measures that had till then created harmony and concord were, somehow or other, lost, dislocated. In Akhenaten's face was refracted the world of that time, like a beam of light in water, appearing twisted and broken. Only it, that face, remained undistorted.

Thirstily he absorbed the features of his chosen beauty. Willy-nilly, the artist approximated that most attractive and most radiant face to the features of repulsiveness. Those blasphemous experiments were unnatural; beauty and the beast began truly to make contact, forgetting themselves, one in the other. Here they are, in the museum showcases, here Nefertiti, here Akhenaten, the princess and the monster, one knows not which is which. For the profile of Nefertiti needs only a slight shading for it to become bestially ugly, to merge into its opposite.

The strangest thing of all in Akhenaten's heresy is that all his monotheism was neither new nor far distant from the Egyptian spirit. It had already been preached in the earliest dynasties; the face of Aten shone from the walls of tombs in early Sakkara. The three Amenophis, the great-grand-father, grandfather, and father of Akhenaten, preached it. There was always *one* god—fractioned, it is true, into certain of his aspects and symbols. Why then did Akhenaten's ideas have such an earthquake effect, an effect that rocked the canons of the monumental kingdom? Because it was a monster who announced them, so that they appeared monstrous, bizarre, irresistible.

Hundreds of books and studies have been devoted to the enigma of Akhenaten and Nefertiti. But whoever stumbles upon the Akhenaten room in the Cairo museum will be convinced that the tales of this spiritual revolution may best be discerned through the eyes of the artist. From these sculptures, from these reliefs in clay or granite, beams the true chronicle, the events of which there is no record, for even the participants themselves were not aware of them. Watching how beauty slowly becomes thin and dissolves like a cloud in too strong sunlight, we realize what sort of terrible drug Akhenaten was in his time. Seeing painter and sculptor driven to frenzy, to hatred, seeing how they dispossess the face of the Pharaoh of every trace of humanity, every rich-ness, seeing how even the god-inspired Thuthmosis no longer knows what is beauty, we see that the whole period gazes into that horror face as if obsessed, not knowing whether in the next moment to spit on it in disgust or to merge into it bewitched.

In some portraits a most satanic smile hovers around those fleshy, female lips. A less ugly Pharaoh would not have succeeded. That ugliness which sang of the most beautiful things hypnotized his times. The ideas he preached would not have struck so powerfully, nor, after his death, would everyone have turned their backs on him in rage had not the supreme monster stood behind them. Nor would the art of Amarna have burst out as if in fever, nor the most beautiful woman of Egypt have faded, transformed into a monster.

AMULETS

UDJAT

That is the eye of the sun, the eye of the falcon, the eye
of the god Hor (Horus). It is drawn as a protective symbol
on all sarcophagi to ensure that the gaze of the gods rests on
the souls of the dead. Countless ceramic, glass, jeweled, and
golden eyes gleam in the darkness of the sarcophagus. Sewn
amid the mummy wrappings, Lilliputian charms peep out
from the rings on the withered fingers, and pendants rest
on the blackened breasts of the dead. For the ignorant the
udjat is a charm against the evil eye; for those who know,
it is the gaze that penetrates the illusion of time and space.
For the gaze of the gods is all-seeing—a horizon seen from
a point where there is no longer space or time, where everything is here and now and forever.

Where is the point that cancels our dual chimera, time and
space—two vessels near one another that, though empty, unceasingly pour from one to the other? The Egyptian adepts
knew that it was within us. They also knew that the way
to it is dangerous—for the uninitiated, the fall into the abyss,
deeper and darker than the heavens, is certain. The priests
jealously guarded this secret of esoteric learning. It died with
their caste. Inexplicable symbols remain: the knot of Isis
(*tyet*), the pillar of Osiris (*djed*), the circle of eternity and
symbol of life (*ankh*), and the eye of the great seer (*udjat*).

The eye of the great seer is within us, closed and lulled to sleep. The eye that opens in another reality, suddenly and directly, just as the eye of the sleeper opens in the morning twilight. Time that we "spend" is immeasurable by the time of our ordinary sight. The moment we have "passed" is where we have always been! *Udjat* is our link between the moment and eternity, a handshake between that time in which we die and that time in which we are immortal.

ANKH

My life is the effort I make to resist death. *Ankh* tells us: life does not resist anything that is not itself. What it resists are changes within itself.

I don't know what *ankh* is. I don't know what life is. But I know that only it exists and nothing else.

TYET

In the ash of an Egyptian village squats Iset, the patient weaver. She squats and weaves her blood and ties it in a knot; that knot is *tyet*. And so knotted, the blood flows from heaven to earth, upward and downward, linking the four corners of the earth and the seven mighty winds between them. The knot is a woman's face, so like *ankh*, as if it were its twin sister of unchanging life. It was Izida, the village herb gatherer, who first sniffed hemlock and snake poison and the healing taste of bitterness; it was Iset who lay in wait for the mucus and excrement of the gods, to mingle and knead them into asps and the Augean paths of life.

O gay palaces have you no inkling that the strings of your welcoming harps tighten on the farther side the gallows' nooses? On the threshing floors of the Egyptian villages squats the raven-faced hag, the gap-toothed Madwoman; she squats and weaves her blood, then threads it through the hollow tooth she found when scratching in the ash, sewing together good and evil, remedy and poison, heaven and earth, me and Myself. That is the same stealthy Mokoš who writhes in the Slav mire, in the soul of the white Neva Nevičica (Princess Snowflake).

And the knot, that is a woman's face so like *ankh*, as if it were a twin sister who conceived and gave birth to him, her eternal father.

VIGNETTE FROM "THE BOOK OF THE DEAD"

"I am your sister Isis, the divine mother," says the goddess on the left. She kneels under the cupola of heaven, her knees on the cushions of the dawn, and bows to the *djed*, the spine of Osiris which supports the sun. Facing Isis her sister Nephthys kneels, her knees on the cushions of the dusk, and humbly, as if to implore the dead king's memory, murmurs: "I am your sister Nephthys."

Ah, we know Isis well, we know Nephthys well. Who was it lured the red-haired Set to begin that loathsome fratricide? Who holds the threads of the three-handed plot, who in her knot weaves the killer and his victim, and afterward weeps with the widow on the fields without harvest? Your good king, Osiris-Agamemnon, Father of Thy Only Son Hamlet—Father of Thy Only Son Orestes—Father of Thy Only Son Horus—bores you to death. We follow you as we walk down the steps into history, and, descending, you become smaller—yet always still the royal vampire, though punished by your sons, who no longer recognize in you their own, but their father's mistress.

The spirit of dawn and the spirit of dusk gaze at one another, face to face. Between them rises the spinal column of the sun, the stalk on which sways the heavy sunlit flower. Who is who here, crucified between contradictions? Only one unique soul; tortured by its monstrous richness.

Isis is that stem and Isis is that flower. Isis is her own

repentant sister. Isis is the raging murderer, Isis is the dis-membered victim of her own intrigue, Isis is the mother who will bear her own impregnator. Isis is the voracious spider tormented by the unexpended poison of tenderness. Her left hand is Set and her right Osiris; with the left she kills and with the right restores life.

So spins the great wheel of the universe, now to one, now to the other side. The drunken chakra of Maha-maya, the lion of yesterday and the lion of tomorrow devouring one another, yang and yin growing one into the other.

It is always the same story of the stride of the world, of the tottering double stride, which never gets anywhere.

EGYPT

*Was it by chance that they revered the flower
of the water lily; was it by chance they recognized
in the lotus the features of their land?*

Take a stick and draw a lotus in the sand, on its long, gently curved stem. Then, in fact, you will have drawn the Nile. Then, in fact, you will have drawn Egypt.

Through the sand meanders the stem of the Nile, seen through the eyes of a passenger in a plane. Swaying gently, as if the desert currents impel it, it flowers in its delta and, incised by two main streams shot through with blue veins, spreads out, petal-like, to meet the Mediterranean.

The stem droops and plunges through the sands of the wilderness until somewhere near Khartoum it touches the frontiers of a different land and is suddenly torn asunder, as its two main streams plunge deep into the darkness of Africa.

The stem forces its way through the water lilies; it rises through the sands of three deserts, through four gorges of cataracts; finally, it totters around the bluff of Dendera, bending its knees like a pensive ibis, and then straightens out, touched by the distant magnet of its crown.

But it is not enough to bend over an atlas. One must see also the speeded-up film of the millennia. In that film the huge, slow watery mass quivers in the wind of time; the centuries ripple its clear face, pushing its pliant stem now right now left.

The Nile shines, scarcely perceptibly green, its raging torrent trembling, trembling as if with awe, for in the next moment the red-hot sword of the sun will cut it short. It cools the surface of the perspiring plants, and that dewy outline, that green vapor, is the live, the unchanging, the real Egypt, her thirty million souls, her threefold harvest years imprinted five thousand times in the dark silt. That is her Pharaohs, sultans, kings, and presidents; there like a fata morgana gleam her cities and her cemeteries, her dams and her temples, her wars and her truces, her enigmas and her eternity. All past, present, and future, Egypt is, when one looks at it from above, only an aura of the radiant and immortal Nile lotus.

Sapling of living water, you sway through the motionless fire of death. Nowhere in the world are there such harmoniously formulated conflicts; for you are a print of the blue flower of heaven, its shadow on earth, on the devil's skin. Your breath is living beings. They evaporate in the flaming nostrils of the sun.

Life-giving sapling, how you rustle through the deadly threefold silence of the deserts. You writhe upward like the blind, sinewy sap, later to burst into flower, awareness, and beauty. The tremor that enwraps you, the scent that overpowers you, that is our flesh and all its hopes of immortality. Nowhere on earth are there such harmoniously formulated conflicts; for you are the signature of the most fertile hand in the greatest barrenness of earth.

DESERT SERMON

Man is a window into himself; and man is a landscape that gazes through it.

Man needs nothing other than what he has; and he who has received the desert as his lot is as rich as he who rejoices in the jungles of Yucatan. For whatever one has is enough for the creative game of recognizing Oneself around oneself: and there is no aridity on earth where there are not countless signs of the power of the creator. Nor is there any landscape in which man does not reveal the grammar of his eternal spirit.

The desert, at first unrewarding and monotonous, nourishes in its peoples a special ability to discern subtle distinctions. In that, the desert Arab is the equal of the most silken Chinese brush. He moves slowly, almost like a woman, among the variants of spiritual desires; and these nuances are as incalculable as the shifting colors of the sand dunes. Probably no Indo-European language has such a wealth of conceptions for changes of mood and personality as are to be found in the language of the Arabian desert. Nowhere such hedonistic abundance on an irrational emotional scale: nowhere such deeply felt shades of mood, so much respect for individual fancies and cravings, as in those men who in their countless generations have wandered through these landscapes without astonishment.

Things and events are rare in the desert; one's gaze drinks them in greedily, enjoying the flow of thought and form which are to be found in even the most uncomfortable of them. Whoever has been even on the edge of the sands can see how tender and misty their colors are, how harsh and sharp their outlines. In truth, it is this many-faceted brotherhood of clarity and vagueness that distinguishes the maturity of Arab thought.

Carved in that landscape, like a cameo in stone, stands that magnificent beast the camel. It has learned its swaying gait from the desert; nothing is more wavelike than the springing of the sandy dunes under its feet. From the desert also it has learned its impassivity; nothing is stiller than the noonday sun over the desert and the camel's absent-minded gaze fixed on the horizon. In the meager alphabet of the desert, the camel is the most eloquent and the most luxurious letter.

The desert Arab passes half his life on the camel's back. He listens with his whole body to the rhythm of the camel's swaying, an intricate and monotonous rhythm upon which his survival depends. The camel bears the litter with the beautiful girl, and the warrior in his most frenzied charge. It gives its skin, its hair. The contact of distant civilizations across the sandy wastes is inconceivable without the camel. It has become the standard of comparison, the symbol of virtue. In Arabic poetry there are over a hundred famous analogies for beauty, strength, speed, endurance, nobility, perseverance, and loyalty. But there is no beast which has made for itself so basic a place in the metaphors of national poetry as the camel—not the peacock, not the dove, not the swan; none has been so incomparable, such a model of beauty and other virtues.

Not enough has yet been written about the camel's gait, though it has given its rhythm to Arab poetry and music, to the thought of the desert peoples. The camel is like a music box, in which every tiny cog turns with its own rhythm and its own speed. The music thus composed sounds incomprehensible to a European ear. That ear hears only fragments; the long arpeggios of the camel's neck, the melodious melismata of its spine, the clipped staccato of its tail. (Nothing is easier for the musician than to orchestrate the camel's gait. Nothing is simpler for the mathematician than to express the camel's gait in formulae.)

Its swaying is complex; it is a calm majestic undulation, it is a syncopation where each pair of legs breaks the rhythm of the other pair and the neck swings independently of the limbs. At full speed the camel's body seems almost motionless, like a halted wave against a background of fast-moving landscape. In all the various modes of swaying the camel's "expression" is absent-minded. See with how much enjoyment the stallion's head translates the mad onrush of its muscles! Yes, the Arab horse is yet one more letter, fiery and unrestrained, neither indifferent nor supernatural, discordant, simple. The depth of the stallion's enjoyment is joy itself, is magnificent, but is not more intense than the dreamy indifference with which the camel's head slides into the lead in some Bedouin race.

Not much was needed to teach the camel all that, to become all that. Only a little endless desert. To be where one could see as far as eye can reach, where it is silent and where there is nothing to touch. Something like the sky, merciless and immeasurable, through which wander the drops of living water in the weak, compassionate cases.

Nor is anything more necessary to the desert than some modest infinity, such as the human spirit, so that it, this devil's empty pasture, becomes transformed into wealth. The man who has received the desert as his gift has received enough to make him great, happy, and rich. Just as great, as happy, and as rich as he who finds his pleasure in the dark silt of Egypt. For anything is sufficient for man to make him recognize his inner greatness, happiness, and wealth, just as anything is sufficient to make him forget his own great, happy, and rich environment.

Carved in man as a cameo in stone, the landscape glitters like the mind of man. Nothing is more spiritual than the desert, the virgin forest, the dried wadis, the fountain, the unpicked palms, sand, shade, dew, sunlight, anything. For man's riches seek any form to become visible; any path to the place where they already are.

The sermon of the desert, the sermon of the virgin forest, the sound is the same and always: a self-created spirit.

Rich to the degree to which others and otherness cannot give him; happy to the degree to which his surroundings cannot take it away from him. Man.

THE SERPENT'S SURNAME

How long will I think that I am not you?

Down the narrow serpentine Khan Khalili alley a young woman with sparkling sapphire eyes was walking. She moved strangely, as if without legs, with the gliding rhythm with which a mature snake casts its skin. She dragged behind her the multicolored slough of the street, a skin woven with the diagrams of the shops.

I knew that young woman; she had come to Cairo from Belgrade to study Egyptology. She often used to visit me and we sat together on the terrace in the evening breeze and combed out the Book of the Dead. She was one of those rare beings who can respect their own intuition even if it conflicts with advantageous interpretations. One of those precious and dying-out seekers who believe in the inner voice and don't ask its origin, but follow it devotedly into unexpected terrains where it's so easy to destroy all knowledge and lack of knowledge acquired after long travail. Listening keenly to that inner voice, she understood it—despite her hard-boiled surroundings—as her first and true calling.

We saw one another, therefore, often, but now, in this chance meeting when I, too, was hurrying, though in the opposite direction, I saw her afresh, as a different person. She was that holy Egyptian asp which comes regularly to drink milk in the temple. She had sloughed off the generations and unerringly found her way to the same hospitable threshold. That day I saw her bewildered; her instinct had led her to the right place but the temple was no longer there. Everywhere about her lay the skins of her long-past pilgrimages, serpent traces in the sand, little piles of dark-blue snake sapphires. She recognized all that through her long memories, focused as if into a tip of a tail. This place was the place of meeting, but neither temple nor priests appeared. I watched, suddenly irritated, as she circled around and wiped out her own trail, for she had come trustfully, but something on the other side had intervened.

All that I understood at that moment, and at that moment I took her by the hand, probably to shake her out of that set rhythm. But she slipped away and pointed into the depths of the little street, whispering: "I am in a hurry. . . . Down there, someone wants to show me . . ." and slithered off.

Who wanted to show her, and what? Obviously she was seeking the threshold of her temple, her ration of milk. She thought that she wanted to get to know the old sheik who was sewing a Pharaonic fresco from a mosaic of old rags, or to see the entrails of an Aladdin's cave of copper handicrafts, or perhaps some whirling dervish, or even the banned *zar*, a dance for the exorcism of evil spirits. Perhaps she thought that. But, her tail raised like an antenna, knew that the goal was different, that the promise was more solemn.

I felt as if I had, by chance, found out the surname of some person, the surname that reveals his tribe and his place of origin. So, then, she was a holy snake, a slender dweller in the sand, which crawls to its abode from an alien soil. Where now is that one who with bare hand took her grief and hid it within herself?

I saw her slither irascibly as she crossed her own traces and after some time returned to me to drink black Nubian tea together. Where now is that bare heel that for thousands of years nourished her with milk? And, not knowing, everything around us craved an answer.

A few more such vain loyalties and she will find her poison.

A DREAM OF WILD BEASTS

*In your last letter you ask me what I feel when
writing an "essay" on the Sphinx. What does one feel
writing, with hair standing on end, about wild
beasts, the huge dream-creating wild beasts?*

From a letter to Azra

CONCLUSION

The face of the Sphinx is a prophetic face; but not the face
of a prophet who with foam on his lips calls upon his people
for a rebirth. It's not its wish to transmit its vision. It is so
preoccupied with its own vision that the percipient onlooker
can gather nothing from it; nor can those who have no inkling, and those are ourselves. Here there is, therefore, nothing
save the act of looking; both the enlightened and the unenlightened fall away, and also the desire stretching between
them in both directions. Even that which was seen falls
away; there remains only a great blinding light: vision, infinite vision. Therefore to us the Sphinx appears blind.

If only we don't give up in the first few centuries, we
shall glimpse the place where the beast of the universe has
concealed its strength; but we shall not glimpse that strength.
Peeling one after the other the weaker spots we shall reach
the place where the power of the Sphinx and the solution
of its riddle are centered. O place, O place, O most evident
place, visible to the most naked eye! For the riddle of the

Sphinx is not in her withdrawal into pure vision, but in her stare at that everyday spectacle of the world—the rising sun. So unexceptional a vision for such a unique blindness! For five thousand years or more the Sphinx and the eastern sun have been involved with one another; what is the sun to her, what is she to the sun, that more than one million, seven hundred and twenty-five thousand times they have absorbed one another? *

Thus, after the first few centuries, it dawns on us that we must look at the sun if we wish to understand the Sphinx. Then we look at the sun, at the most everyday spectacle in the world; and if we don't give way it will release in us that transcendent reason for our gaze. We shall release reason for reason, every reason for reason that is not the sun, including the Sphinx. Peeling ourselves thus, we shall not even notice that there are no more outcries of wonder—what am I to the sun, what is the sun to me? Finally, it will happen all at once that we shall release even the sun itself, in order to liberate the great blinding light which is without source and without symbol and without onlookers.

TWO OR THREE IRRELEVANT
HISTORICAL MEETINGS

But when is "all at once?" And who are those in the world who know how to look at the Sphinx? To look at the sun? To look at the light? Thoth's initiates could, the white brotherhood of Kemen could; the alchemists knew, and so did the interpreters of dreams and those who drew up the philosophical systems. Atlantids, Lemurians. The builders of the earliest pyramids knew. By their mystic geometry they created the theoretical runway for the take-off of the spirit for

* The sun is nothing to her, she is nothing to it; the desire that exists between them desires only itself, and does not know it. The desire between them deceives itself with the face of the sun on the heavenly side and on the earthly with the face of the Sphinx. For that desire likes to be deceived; it prefers not to know.

the ascent into the region "where the thought returns from, its mission unaccomplished." The Sphinx was the imprint of that ascent.

Legions and legions of newcomers into the Nile valley didn't know; legions and legions believed blindly in the power of the Sphinx. That blind faith in her power multiplied copies which imitated what was inessential and which alone could be copied. In the case of the Sphinx that meant an unusual composition of human, animal, and divine. However, the other sphinxes were without mystery. The mystery could not be imitated, it had to be innate.

Several times the people of the Nile forgot the strange enormous animal, several times she was buried in the sand to the top of her skull. And several times chosen dreamers dug her out.*

Legions and legions of newcomers to the Nile valley did not know how to understand the Sphinx. They knew that they were frightened of the Sphinx and felt terribly insignificant before her paws, but her clairvoyance they could not perceive. Nor were the savage, extrovert warriors who galloped from the sands of Arabia into the valley of the most

---

* Between the giant paws, higher than a man's stature, rises a small commemorative plaque of black basalt which the Pharaoh Thothmes, fourth of that name, placed there. He put it there about a thousand years after the birth of the Sphinx. The plaque recounts the meeting between the Pharaoh and the Sphinx. It says that Thothmes, when on a hunting trip, wandered away from his companions and, tired out, fell asleep directly above the skull of the buried beast. In a dream the god Harakte appeared to the Pharaoh in the form of the Sphinx and told him: "Dig me out and I will make you king of United Egypt!" It goes on to say that the Pharaoh obeyed his dream; he dug out the Sphinx and established her cult. In return, he became the ruler of united Egypt.

Thothmes's dream was one of the first—if not the first—recorded cases of extrasensory perception. Like a black jewel there rises between the great paws a witness to this vision, this contact in which history and dream recognized one another.

fertile river in the world able to perceive the Sphinx. But the Sphinx knew how not to perceive them; and that unofficial historical clash played, I believe, a great role in their eventual refinement. Ancient Egyptian civilization was by then long dead, but dead in the manner of a dead star whose brilliance still travels through eons and eons of space.

In the twenties of the seventh century the violent explosion of Islam began to spread through the Near East and it spread so self-confidently and fiercely that everything retreated before it, everything was delivered over to it in advance, destined to be destroyed or transformed. In the year 624 at Bedar, near Mecca, a miracle occurred which definitely set the seal on the mental outline of the newborn Islamic society. That was the absurd victory of three hundred followers of Mohammed over a thousand veteran warriors of the Koreish tribe. After that miracle others followed, a no less strange conquering bravura by which the onrush of Islam became transformed into a sudden and delirious breakthrough which has no parallel in history. Neither men nor gods frightened these Bedouin, or brought into doubt their confidence in their mission.*

* The Christian mentality was formed in trauma because of the martyrdom and humiliation of its Founder; this obsession with guilt and sin has bedeviled Christian spirituality for two thousand years. Nor were any later triumphs of the King's regents able to assuage that original pain; neither their power nor their omnipotence was able to conquer this weakness in Christian souls, the shame of the apostles, the sense of remorse of the powerless and frightened, whose supreme Saviour, in the childhood of their world, was spat upon before their very eyes.

The Islamic world, on the other hand, is conceived in glory, through the victory of a handful of true believers in the aura of Mohammed's statesmanship and political success. The choice of the date that begins the Mohammedan era displays its characteristic preference for earthly achievements, for that was the year of the creation of the Islamic state and not the year of the Prophet's birth or of his first inspiration. As a counterexample let us recall how Buddhist pupils learn to choose the holiest point in the universe; it is not the place of Siddhartha's birth

When, therefore, those god-possessed and magnificent conquerors galloped into the already shattered land of the Copts, they caught their breath before the stark appearance of the Sphinx, which contemptuously didn't even look at them. There are no reports, no poems, about that meeting; no one erected a commemorative plaque. It is probable that the newcomers were not aware of the transformation that overcame them when faced by the majestic ruins of Misir. But some allusions speak even more eloquently than any commemorative stele of what occurred on the Gizeh tableland at the time of the Moslem invasion. For, as it happens, the Arabs named the Sphinx Abu Hol, the Father of Terror.*

They were neither Syrians nor Greeks, to know in advance that one of the Seven Wonders of the World awaited them in Egypt. They burst in, unprepared; the fever of jihad by which they had been armed could not withstand the silent merciless blow of its magnificence. They wandered around

---

or death, it is not the hour of the foundation of the monastic order, but the shade of the pipal where from Siddhartha he became the Buddha, where man awoke from the dream of samsara—from that dream in which even the gods sleep, the endless cycle of birth, death, and rebirth.

Obviously that question by the Angel of the Lord on the eve of the decisive battle of Kosovo—which kingdom will you choose, the earthly or the heavenly?—was only rhetorical. For it was put long before the battle, and long before the battle had received its answer. By our life it was asked, by our life it was answered. Let's not ask what someone thinks, let's ask how someone lives. Mohammed and the Moslems lived their fever of jihad (the Holy War) fiercely, conquering one after another the astonished kingdoms of the world. And because of these very down-to-earth reasons, Islam radiated supremacy and assurance in its magnetic belt, from the Atlantic to the mouths of the Ganges.

* Perhaps this quotation from the Book of the Dead fits best of all: "I am Today for countless men and peoples. I am one who has defended you for millions of years; so, whether you be denizens of heaven or earth, whether you live in the south or in the north, fear of me is in your bones" (Theban recension XLII, 19-20).

the Pyramids, trying vainly to dislodge the enormous stone blocks from their resting places in order to build their mosques. The effort was not worth their while. It was easier to cut the living stone from the quarries of Mokattam. It confused them, perhaps even filled them with wonder to be faced by unknown giants who had ruled the world before them.

They feared the Sphinx. There were countless stories of subterranean treasure caves, of which she was the guardian, where every sort of cultural and material treasure from before the Flood was amassed. Even the learned Ibn Battuta wrote: "The Pyramids were built by Hermes to bury in them knowledge, art, and all other achievements from the time before the Great Cataclysm." There were countless tales of evil spirits swarming in the precincts of the Sphinx and wreaking vengeance on the sacrilegious. The tellers of tales again and again told of unseen marvels buried in the entrails of the Great Pyramid. They dreamed, too, of treasures in the environs of the great lighthouse of Alexandria. And when one hotheaded caliph, goaded by tales of treasure, succeeded after frightful labor in boring through the northern wall of the Great Pyramid in the wrong place and by sheer chance drilled his piratical way as far as the true hidden passageway of the old Egyptian builders, there, in the granite funerary chamber hewn in the middle of the pyramid, an empty sarcophagus greeted him.

Sphinx and Pyramids alike filled the greedy raiders with a sense of their own insignificance.* And that imperceptible experience, grafted on the consciousness of being chosen, aroused in the young, just-born society an ability to respect

* Had the Arabs, by some chance, moved first toward the European steppes instead of toward the most imposing civilization of the Mediterranean basin, which, although a ruin, cast its spell with its dead millions, there is every reason to believe that the progress of Arab civilization would have been slower and more painful to the neighboring peoples.

others different from it—which is probably the basic sign of civilization. With ill humor and uneasiness they left in peace both Sphinx and Pyramids, since they could not surpass them as they had surpassed their own predecessors, the wonderful Arabia Felix.

Much later, at the time of the zenith of Arab culture on Egyptian soil, many Arab writers and historians tried their hand on the dark infidel centuries of ancient Egypt. And when, in these flights, they touched on the Sphinx and the Pyramids, their reports had an aroma of pious and childish superstition, with the flavor of enchantment of the *Arabian Nights*, the *Layle alf layle*. How pleasant and touching that transformation of fact-loving chroniclers into dream-makers and visionaries whom fussy pedants don't believe. So, filled with rapture, we must abandon Arab meetings with ancient and glorious Egypt. Let us conclude with two or three little-known manuscripts.*

* The manuscripts in the British Museum edited by the famous Al-telemsan (add. 5927, 7319) mention the subterranean passage linking the Great Pyramid, the Sphinx, and the Nile. In the same manuscripts is noted a marvelous event from the time of Ibn Tulun, which is permeated by the naïve caliph's daydream of the fabulous treasure inside the Great Pyramid. Here is the story:

In the time of Ahmed ben Tulun, a group of men entered the Great Pyramid. In one of the chambers they found a crystal goblet of unusual color and quality. As they were leaving, they noticed that one of their band was missing, so they turned back to look for him, and he appeared before them as naked as when he came from his mother's womb, and said to them: "Do not follow me, do not search for me" and once again disappeared into the pyramid. They realized that their companion had been enchanted and told Ahmed ben Tulun of everything. He then forbade any entry into the pyramid, took the goblet, gave it to be weighed and discovered that its weight always remained the same, were it full or empty.

Another Arab writer, Muterdi, also reports on the fantastic happenings in the entrails of the Great Pyramid. A few adventurers, searching for the subterranean passages of the pyramid, crawled into a low, narrow trench where currents of fresh air greeted them from cleverly

NEOBARBARUS

But there are ignoramuses even more dangerous than the imaginative conquerors from the East. They come in learned hordes, very distinguished, mostly of the species *Neobarbarus evropeisensis*. No one can deny their respect for an alien past—but they classify that past as a childhood of the spirit in a simple and primitive world.

The Sphinx, Mahapurusha or Zervan by their shape give the mind an opportunity to stand humbly aside and let those who are wiser pass. That "deference to the wise" is a sign that the mind has freed itself from the brakes that prevent its flight toward far horizons "where thought returns from, its mission unfulfilled." The strength of the symbol is that to some extent it makes any reasonable intervention impossible; that it excites us to extrasensory perception, the essential sight of man. He who is afraid of such cortical anesthesia will never sufficiently relax to be able to perceive in the Sphinx, Mahapurusha or Zervan his own unlimited consciousness. The inhibited *Neobarbarus* does that systematically, industriously, and efficiently; he leaves in his wake armies of historical mirrors, texts, lectures, and treatises.*

---

placed air ducts. Suddenly, or so Muterdi affirms, the walls moved and cut one man off from his fellows. Later, the lost man once again appeared, but spoke to them in some unknown language.

* O Doctor Ignorantia! In truth the most established amongst all the other ignoramuses, the most influential, the most dangerous—a real spiritual drought. In such a deadly clime some will yearn naïvely for pure and unsullied ignorance, for an enchanting lack of education, which does not fall into the trap of learned nonsense. They will yearn for it, they will yearn for it as for the blessed Earthly Paradise. They will yearn—and thereby deceive themselves. For, while he was a pure and unsullied ignoramus, man did not enjoy that condition, for he was not conscious of it. He gave it the sobriquet of bliss only after he had gambled it away for something far less worthy, for an undigested mouthful of the apple of knowledge.

GLORIOUS AND INGLORIOUS ROTATION

Around the Sphinx a circling of interrupted charm; a dream-like swaying of camels overgrown with tourists; some unrecognized obeisances. (With calm dignity the camels submit to all that alien swarming, immoderate, a blend of heat and fatigue.)

Around the Sphinx one more, wider, consecrated circle, invisible, more refined and more hypnotic than the first; that is the magnetic ring forged from the thoughts of dreamers, priests, philosophers: an unintentional *opus circulatorium*.

A magnificent dance, an ecstatic dance, a fairy dance—and very dangerous. For whosoever is caught up in it easily forgets around what he is moving; the snake of the dance deceives him and erases from his mind the precious stone in the middle, erases from his mind that middle which cannot be touched by any other mind but only by his own being. That seductive and glorious rotation is one of the ruses of the great beast. That is the mandala which the beast has enscribed about itself, that is her flaming veil within which, to her heart's content, she is what she is: Isis, goddess of loneliness.

Yes, it is glorious, it is respectful, to be a part of the ritual circle in which many dead and a few living support one another in their circling around the holy of holies. But the movement that breaks away from the ring of adoration and rushes *toward* the holy of holies, that movement is invisible and solitary, although the horizon is brighter and more populated.

Yes, it is glorious, it is respectful, to choose words of thanksgiving to the Lord and not call upon the heavenly hearing but only upon those mortal listeners who think in a similar way. It is inglorious, it is disrespectful to be a real poet, and to wish to be silent, to be nothing, to be. For the poet's word is trash, the debris from the poet's effort to be silent, to be.

That, about which silence keeps silent, is the subject of our talk about the Sphinx.

LAPIS NILOTICUS

*Green bough, green bough which I have
not planted in my heart!
Bird, songbird, which braids its
nest on that bough!
Song, song to which I listen, yes, song
to which I listen!*

Writing this, I don't begin, but continue, a painful, torturing task: the collection of my own fragments which have been scattered in space after a long-past heliocentric cataclysm. I don't know if my labors will prove of value as "literature." For they are first and foremost a therapeutic account of travel through undimensional lands where rules the ancient alchemist principle that darkness is illuminated by darkness. Also I don't know who it is who sends me on this task of collection, but clearly I am a robot under direction, capable of translating, for better or worse, the signals of my command center.

When the link between the controller and the robot is broken, alternatively when the receiving apparatus goes wrong, we call it spiritual breakdown. The disconnected rocket rushes out of its orbit into the field of alien gravitation and reflects on its shattered screen swarms of signals which break through on their way to other targets.

Many times I have tried to turn in the direction where

these signals come from, a direction contrary to my advance. But every unconscious, unskilled movement is dangerous and may easily dislocate the delicate joints of our contacts. Two or three times my capsule has tilted uncomfortably, the compass needle has turned about its axis, and everything that I call "me" has found itself engaged in feverish effort to regain its former equilibrium. Now I ask myself if it isn't worthwhile to obey the ancient counsel given to those who travel into the unknown: don't turn your head, don't look back. Later, when Orpheus has left the underworld, let him turn freely to his own saved soul. Isn't that, really, the archetypal principle by which man must, first of all, trustfully and patiently carry out his task, however petty and insignificant, and through that trial grow in stature for the revelation for which previously he was immature? Not to write before he is ready for a poem, as Rilke advises: not to write until he deserves it, by the observation of countless things, things that are worthwhile, things that are insignificant, things that are everyday, external or internal, scattered or collected. Not to try to blossom before the spring. For rewards ripen with man; when Jacob began his service with Rachel's father, a service of twice seven years, Rachel was surely still a child.

One evening, while flying through a very dense signal area which in my diary I called *Egypt*, the premonition was born in my robot soul that I should turn to my own controller through his own devices. In my travel diary I write:

"Before going to bed on the banks of the Nile, I turned to my wiser and invisible colleague and begged him to show himself to me in dream. I pressed the key that enables me to receive his messages. I headed my petition *To Him* and not *To Myself* for, though obviously we were two ends of a single sound, the distance between us is far too great for us to be called 'I.'"

That night I dreamed of the little spiral house of a snail. It was a sea snail, a great extinct shape from the Carboniferous age. I felt the turning movement as a gentle eddy; at first the ripple gently drew me upward toward the pointed apex, but at the same time I tore myself free of the spiral, frightened. It seemed to me that in that spasm I awakened myself and immediately after that plunged into dream, into the spiral. The snail, a living nebula, raised its circular tower like an eddy turned upward. Once more I felt overwhelmed by the gentle spiral and once again, like a distrustful, inexperienced swimmer, broke free. And thus again several times until the image faded.

Only after a few days did I become conscious that the form and movement of the spiral snail were an authentic and accurate picture of that inner center which I had been trying to confront. Such a metaphor of the atman I had nowhere either seen or read. The source of being is represented in India by the symbol of the lotus, the spider in its web, the center point of the wheel; in China by the crystal cube, alias the diamond solid; and in medieval Europe by the symbol of the scholar-mystics, the *lapis invisibilitis*, the *mystic rose*, the fountain in the walled garden. But the snail, its point turned upward like an inverted maelstrom, obviously originated in my own subconscious interpretation, that is to say in the subconscious workshop wherein incomprehensible reality is transformed in less accurate but more comprehensible symbols.

On one of the following mornings the same symbol aroused me from my emotional and intellectual routine when visiting a school of painters on the cape of the island of Rhoda. The school, which demanded that its participants respect traditional forms, especially Arabic ornamentation, looked like a monastery, a place of arid sterility and rancid fantasy. We dragged along, from exhibit to exhibit, distressed in soul, till I became aware of the majestic signals of an exceptionally large sea snail behind the glass of one of the showcases. The students didn't know where the snail had come from: it had probably come from the Red Sea, rich in hypertrophied forms of the long-lost Tethys. Some discerning teacher had placed

114

the snail among the students' carvings as a pedagogic admonition that nature, that is to say unschooled life, is the most gifted of all sculptors. Every sector was composed of countless delicate limestone threads. The life which at one time had crouched at the bottom of that web had wound in spiral threads, at first vertiginously dense and later expanding in ever slower and wider coils.

A night or two after that first dream I dreamed another, cunningly patched together from the tatters of a banal fantasy. A girl friend of mine from Zagreb and I found ourselves in a car which was to take us to some shadowy destination. I had the impression that it was a rendezvous of some sort, in a house with its front overgrown by vines. At the wheel sat a Negro in a white shirt; Zora was sitting beside him, and I on the back seat. She seemed to have known him before and apparently knew where we were going and why, for she explained to me that the Negro had a friend, or maybe a brother, whom we were to meet. Also, the whole expedition was in some way linked with my son's illness, for I had a vague idea that the black driver was a doctor. He was silent all the time, his back turned toward me, which made me feel a little uneasy. As the car moved on, I felt again that gentle, circular movement.

Next morning I wrote off that dream as something without meaning. But the image of the black driver seen only as the back of a white shirt, so silent and mysterious, began to rise before me as a sign that wouldn't let itself be disregarded. The dark-colored chauffeur driving me to an unknown destination and whose face I had never been able to see, the swan in my psychic Tuonela, was an autonomous function of my own subconscious, its leaning toward the mean. My friend, who behaved as go-between, and who, like the chauffeur, knew where we were going, must represent a semiconscious activity that links the ego with the depths of being. The sick son (who recovered from his illness, though traces remained in his lungs) most probably meant some newborn part of my psyche, badly damaged by my apathy. But what connected that dream with the one that came before was that unerring circular movement, that gentle vertigo which was a magnetic symptom of a present yet concealed mean.

Clearly I must draw the final lesson. The subconscious processes led me, therefore, toward the desired mean. There was no direct contact between my consciousness and that other inner process; we needed a mediator, a go-between, a copula, a translator. The mediator might be a poem, something written, a robot travel diary. The dream showed me that only in that irregular manner was it possible for me to get into touch with the unknown chauffeur, with the Virgil-Hermes-Anubis, who was also the doctor of the cancerous part of my psyche. But who was that casually mentioned comrade or brother of the black psychopomp who would perhaps join us? With this question I entered that sector of my reality which at the touch of my electrode dissolved like smoke.*

Two or three nights after the second dream I had a third. In it, I walked through a shallow stream somewhere on the outskirts of the primeval forest. The water swarmed with snakes and baby alligators. Someone near me said in a warning voice that he could summon other and larger animals and someone repeated that "he was in touch with them." The ford which I had first been told was "shallow" sank under my feet and became filled with mini-monsters. It was, in fact, Charon's stream, the boundary of the underworld. Someone within me held on a leash a monstrous denizen of the deeps.

---

* That urge of ours to decipher everything, to bring everything into the open! More often it is a sign of intellectual conceit than a serious and devoted longing. More often it is the desire to overcome than the desire to surrender.

It's necessary simply not to understand certain things for us to be able to accept them and make use of them. The dream that we can resolve once and for all—like a rebus or a charade—would lose its enchantment for us, its therapeutic and prophetic value.

I marveled at the readiness with which the dream replied to my questions. As one of the next "replies," I caught sight of the miraculous *lapis*, the supreme substance for which man searches so intensively in the laboratory and in his own soul. The *lapis* appeared as a nondescript spongy lump. It looked like a barley loaf. Then the lump began to disintegrate into crumbs. I saw hands all about me stretching out for them, and someone explained to me that anyone could take a piece.

I must come into closer contact with sunken masters and their heralds. Between me and my axis there are a number of layers, whirlpools, and circles, each of which has its denizens and its weird rules. Their pictorial telegrams used to arrive worded in various tongues, expressed in various letters and various handwritings. But I was not ripe enough to solve their riddles, patiently and confidently to decipher them.* But I impatiently turned within myself, twisted into an unnatural position, striving to by-pass the strata of millions of years. The moral slowly crystallizes; no vertical climb can evade the natural way to advance, the gentle vertigo. A breakneck leap toward the source would provoke a psychic catastrophe.

Therefore I noted down in my diary "the answer" from the center: *The aim is what you collect on the way to it.* It was an excellent diagnosis of my long-forgotten malady, of my impatient heedlessness of everything that was not final and supreme. The rose—so tapped out my key—is what grows out of the dark roots and the unflowering thorns; the lotus is what whitens out of the mud and silt of the marshes.

That violent thrust upward—didn't it scorch all my loves in the seed? Didn't I begin to love like someone opening a game of chess with the queen, ignoring the existence of the pawns? As soon as someone's face took my fancy, I would already live through my flight upward, breaking the spindle

* Let no one go to Jung or to some witch woman for an interpretation, however greatly he is bewildered by his dreams. Let everyone interpret his own dreams, for everyone sends his own dreams to himself; everyone, therefore, holds the key to their interpretation.

of the sun and the moon, making all God's world unnecessary. It's not the same to hurl oneself upward and to climb there by the spirals that coil under the bark of the tree, pressing onward to the living crown. The summit is not the same in both cases; he who climbs upward like a trunk, bearing on his shoulders the rings of age and the spiral tree-tops, builds his own summit by climbing to the crown where the sun is ripening. He who only hurls himself upward, cutting across the rings of growth, will measure the height of the trunk by his own impatience, with a short measure. Hadn't I squandered all my loves even before they had begun?

The aim is what you collect in your knapsack on your way to it, under your own skin.

In my knapsack I had already collected a hundred or so fragments, impressions, some ashes, some faded colors and canvases. But who will assemble all this litter into a nucleus of an image which resembles me? And how will he do it? For, as the shrewd alchemists know well, the most perfect work is that which is similar to oneself. The most difficult thing is creating something that is similar to itself.

Insofar as in the control tower they had not even concerned themselves with my robot affairs, the Image, already formed, was maybe already waiting for me at the apex of the spiral. Osiris, made whole, was perhaps awaiting his wife-sister-mother at the end of her wanderings. But that was no reason to cease collecting His fragments.

Let the mystery remain a mystery, the key tapped out. Why bother your head so much about tomorrow when it is enough that tomorrow thinks of you?

But now it is night, night, and I am sending my answers to the messages. Ah, morning, do you think of me as much as I try not to think of you?

What other message should I send to myself? The incomprehensible can only be reached through the incomprehensible.

REFRAIN OF THE ARAB FOUNTAIN

*I travel through my own soul, through the glistening
spaces of the world, I travel in my own small dark
body which fears the light.*

My soul doesn't speak to me. But it offers to me signs to
awaken knowledge buried within me. I don't travel. I don't
look at fresh faces and new cities, but my soul tirelessly
arranges and rearranges its tarot, the living letter of untrans-
latable messages.

Suspecting nothing, I opened my eyes in the scorching
twilight of the Old City of Cairo. The houses here don't turn
their faces but their backs to the world. I pass through the
dust-laden wall, dive into the somber gloom of unbaked
brick, and suddenly I am struck by the sign of silver and of
gurgling, stems of living spray that grow out of the pious
stone. A memory that isn't mine alone tries to break free from
the framework of my little biography. I am a drop that evil
winds have dashed over the wall, over the burning desert.
Return me to the water where I came from, among the drops
not yet spattered. I am the tears of that fountain which
plashes joyfully. I am the blind spot in the eye of the onlooker. I am

that fragment of Myself which has fallen farthest away,
which is the smallest. . . .

The outer wall of the house sees no one, nor wishes to be seen. And inasmuch as it is blind and unlovely, so the inner courtyard is dewy and cool and glistening with the sheen of water. The whole house circles around the courtyard, around the crystal water stem; its windows and all its secret places are open to the courtyard. Its eyes, like the eyes of a mystic, are turned inward. The house revolves around the courtyard, revolves like thirsty mouths, and the faces of those who have lived here for generations are fixed onto that inner space which quenches their thirst.

Of all peoples only the peoples of the waste really know how to breathe freely in a walled space which keeps them divided from the merciless suzerainty of the sun. They are eager for water, for that cool murmuring, these desert wanderers, and the houses they began to build in the lands they conquered were built around little winged fountains, around the magic source of life. The house has the function of a mandala, a closed circle that protects the consecrated water space.

That basic attitude of the Arab house spread through all Islamic Asia, gladly adopted even in districts without deserts. For it meant something far more complex than a mere defense against unfriendly nature; it was the attitude of the Sufi, that Islamic mystic who explores his own soul. The Arab house is the face of a man turned away from the world, from the desertlike and waterless region, and concerned only with his own soul, the life-creating source.

No, I don't travel. I don't observe new faces and cities, but my soul tirelessly copies hieroglyphs which reveal the inmost depths of my experience. No, I don't go on pilgrimages through India, Egypt, and Mesopotamia but I in myself am becoming what I really am. For I saw nothing that I hadn't seen before. I owned nothing that was not already mine. All those fountains, all those ziggurats, all those stupas, and all those obelisks are the emanations of my own depths, and I, swaying on the fragile skiff of my body, name them one by one as they appear on the surface.

The whole source, drop by drop, goes farther from itself and, drop by drop, returns. But the drops don't know; it is the source that knows. They break away, into tendrils of pearl, one by one like beads of a necklace; but the beads don't know what the necklace knows. We are the blind spots in the eye of the onlooker. We are the tears of that fountain which splashes joyfully.

Like an eight-legged glistening spider, the fountain appears in the midst of the octagonal marble basin. It is the image of the soul, the image of the world. Like the eight-petal flower of the medieval *hortus*—the rose of existence—the source appears from its eight jets. It is the image of the world, the image of the soul. Two symbols that have arisen in different civilizations, but that are fundamentally the same and have the same meaning: the octagonal micro- and macro-cosmos.

No, but my soul copies the hieroglyphs of my most ancient experience.

TESTING THE AMULET

When you no longer want proofs, they will come to you themselves, not to be the mother of your belief, but its children.

Grihakuta, the "Eagle's Peak," which rises not far from the old Indian capital Rajagriha—the modern thermal spa of Rajmir—is harsh, quiet, swarming with devoted pilgrims to the stupas, honeycombed with violet-white caverns near the summit. More than two thousand five hundred years ago Gautama Siddhartha, from the northern Sakya tribe, the greatest *tathagata*, lived there immersed in meditation. I clambered up there, in the hope that that far-off, perhaps not yet quite evaporated, presence would reveal to me some understanding, even though the Buddha's thinking seemed to me at that time painful, like the thought of a lingering despair which cannot heal anyone's despair but only intensify it.

I was hunting, therefore, something essential, that conceivable molecule of miraculous aroma left behind, something in the darkest corner of a cavern. The more improbable that fragment, that *sacro speco*, seemed to me, the greater the promise of a full and painless revelation. Perhaps Buddha, or at least Ananda, might have lost his clay cup here; perhaps it fell from his hands as he was descending the steep slope; perhaps in some crevice there still lurked a chip which could whisper to me what he who used to drink from it thought. Here in Cairo, I see that I was, at that time and in that place, really in despair, for he is desperate who seeks salvation from a relic. I made my way upward to the hill, hopeless in the broad daylight, in its transparent, shimmering gold, and I convinced myself that I was fortunate, for he is fortunate who climbs Grihakuta on the scent of the trail of wonders that passed this way two and a half millennia ago.

I am descending Grihakuta to meet myself, dressed in Egyptian cotton mingled with Indian khaddar, Ganesh and Bes touching one another resonantly on my bracelets. "What would be changed," I asked one climbing upward, "should a miracle take place here *today* while you are climbing and I am descending?" The figure in khaddar halted; because of my question she never reached the summit. She remained there on the steep slope, and I, powerless as a relic, nailed to the golden day and fastened to the bracelet of incurable wandering: "You'll never lead anyone home, you miniature gilded climber, petrified by your own future; you'll never bring anyone home as long as you believe in Grihakuta or in Delphi and not in your own ascent to the summit."

No, nothing would be changed were a miracle to pass this way today. Even if all those about me achieved Buddhist consciousness, it would not help me in any way. For everyone attains by himself what is his own, everyone in his own skin, as in a Chinese sack, rolls down the steep slope toward the lake, right to its bottom. Haven't I, often enough in this world, looked on the masks of Buddha and Osiris, those faces looking inward? I have looked at them at Buddh-Gaya, at Thebes, at Ajanta, at Nalanda, in the Cairo museum, at Sarnatha, at Matura, at Ellora; always they have been the gates of paradise, closed and unguarded; for only he who knows can open them, he who deserves to enter, who has his own charms, his own amulet, his own relics. Haven't I sat, equally hopelessly, before living *samanas?* Before Krishna Menon, the teacher of Advaita? His face and voice, filled to the brim with severe peace, didn't open to my frantic knocking. He sat on the banks of the Nile, in a banana grove; below him, around him, hovered a sort of Louis Seize armchair; but he, in that armchair, sat relaxed, a proof of his own starry distance. And the men around that armchair gazed at their teacher as men gaze at the stars. How can one touch a star? I incessantly asked myself in all the words I could remember at the time. "In no way; *become* a star," I was answered, once and for all. "Don't come near me, don't touch me, *be* what I am: truth."

With fingers, with eyes, I traced the boundless, saintly *arahat* features, but they were not unlocked for me. O invisible face, free-floating on the wine of dreams! Even if you offer me your rib, so that I could wind about it like a creeper, yet I would still remain without support. Even had you taken me between your lips and silenced me there, still I would cry aloud for help. No, it's better that I turn my back on you, great Amulet, on you too, godlike Milarepo, and on you, *bhagavans* of Arunchala, and on you, Hermes Trismegistus, Thoth's avatar, and on all of you, *doctores mirabiles*, adepts and seers. The myth is tested but it is not conquered; I have not yet reached into my own heart, but I have set out toward it.

THE ZIGGURAT AT UR

*I look at the night sky and see the peace and order
which I have banished from myself. The night sky
knows what it is doing—and I think that I don't.*

These stars and their skies I had banished from my soul and
then I began to raise observatories, gigantic measuring devices and snares for starry sounds and shadows. Now, as soon
as I touch any of these exiles with astrolabe or telescope,
their scar on the native soil of my soul begins to hurt. For
the innermost sky is full of scars from one-time stars. And
somewhere near the navel of the psychic maelstrom a great
scar shines white; above it at the zenith burns the sun, at the
nadir the summit of the ziggurat of Ur.

One of the most powerful instruments that I constructed
to lay bare my perverted, corrupted soul is certainly this
ziggurat, complex and yet terribly simple, raised on the waves
of the underground megalopolis of Ur. A searing, whitish
wind beats its wings, mingling the hummocks of shattered
potsherds, each hummock clashing with the next; and at the
foot of these hummocks roll golden cups and below these
cups an ancient dream of power—dream collides with dream
and a clash like the clang of swords can be heard. That's Ur,
restless in its grave for five thousand years. Only the ziggurat
is motionless, invulnerable as thought, like the common de-
nominator of all this turmoil.

Yes, like some mathematical skeleton, the ziggurat stands out among the seething graves. By its rhythm the ziggurat poses a problem; it is both restless and dynamic and yet it has the bulk and the immobility of a mountain or some boulder which is not in the mood to play.

Its creators subjected themselves to astronomical determinism, the cruel mechanics of heavenly time. Look at them, they stand around a huge zodiacal dial, Sumerian figures with astonished onyx glances, as helpless on their strong, short legs as if delivered over to someone's deliberate insanity. They stand calmly, though not tranquilly; something uneasy racks their inner selves.

I circle around it, filled with an even greater longing for it than in the days of my Zagreb fantasy, when I, like a conspirator against my own times, read Ceram and Noah Kramer. At that time I felt that only physical distance stood between me and the ziggurat and that I would, in a face-to-face encounter, comprehend, simply and easily, the mystery of its function; even more, that I would, with it as a magnetic needle, come into contact with the vagrant axis of my being. It's ten years since I left Zagreb, ten years in which I've been wandering from stargazer to stargazer, and now, in the shadow of the most gigantic of them, I would more willingly lie in its shade and go to sleep, to dream not of weeping but of laughter. It would be better, it would be best, not to pay any attention to it, to open the picnic basket and eat my fill of Kurdistan apples, then empty my bladder and perhaps even my entrails, stretch my stiffened limbs and return without looking back, without turning—return to Baghdad, to Cairo, to Delhi, to Belgrade, to Zagreb, to Dubrovnik.

Now I see that, like lovers, external distances only bring us closer together.* I begin to envy my one-time faith in the power of everyday space. How freely did I load my sins on

* O separated lovers, proximity is a mortal danger, and yet you hasten to embrace! Here they are, one hurrying from the northern confines of the land, the other from the heavenly hours of the South, hastening to the trysting place long ago agreed, most carefully chosen. With the

its fragile backbone! For it is easy to crack the box of space, to crumple its four sides and flatten it like a handkerchief. But, after that, it is hard to remain naked and unprotected before things that have broken free from their nest of space, threatening their final withdrawal into themselves.

The ziggurat was built to a plan that could best be described as mathematical-prophetic, the system by which Tresmagistus composed his combinations in the tarot, or even Fu Hsi his hexagrams in the *I Ching*.

Archaic buildings, such as the ziggurats, the *intihuatane*, and the Pyramids are raised in strict reliance on the values of earth-sky space; all are placed on carefully chosen sites, just at the point where they are most sensitive to the influences of telluric-cosmic forces. Such a site becomes transformed into a nerve center, from which it is possible to govern the movements of the clouds, the lightning, the rain, the floods, a site where they could be brought into harmony with the orbits of rulers and planets. Insofar as each of these mechanisms was a world of its own, so far it was accurate.

In truth, of all the fantastic buildings that man has raised, the ziggurats are the most fantastic. Their builders made no effort even to provide any sort of veil which might conceal their true intent; the ziggurats are neither the tombs of rulers nor military lookout posts. Apart from a few learned men who had been initiated, what could their contemporaries have thought about the ziggurats? The ziggurat occupied the central position in the city; that position, as well as its dimensions and the labor involved in its construction, all go to show that an exceptionally important building was in question or an

---

swiftness of an arrow I'll draw nearer to the hem of the quivering river where the device of Tammuz's youth has been embroidered. With the swiftness of an arrow they'll come. The arrow is humming, my heart ecstatically awaits you. The ziggurat and I are lovers—if one dares so to call the staff that is continually shortening from both ends. If one so dares to name the beginning and the end which set out and diminish at the same time till the would-be suicides kiss in the middle—ay, my love, you are nothing more than the joy of extinction.

exceptionally important function. For the uninitiated the ziggurat was the bearer of the temple, the platform upon which the gods descended. On its summit rose the lookout station of the skies, that is to say, a holy place. For the unlearned it was the place for pious rituals of thanksgiving and nothing more. For the initiate it was a philosophical-astrological composition, a four-dimensional map, an organization that seized upon and condensed cosmic energy with all its beneficial attributes; some sort of protective umbrella over the city, something like a lightning conductor against evil, something like an interpreter of fate.

Its shape was independent of any practical use. Let's take a well or a bathhouse, a tomb, an altar, or a cradle; all are obviously made to fulfill a function. The nature of the material, sometimes even the features of the landscape, determine variations in form. But the shape of the ziggurat doesn't reveal any definite usage; most frequently it is a cascade of steps, divided by tranquil, ceremonial paved terraces. To reach the summit, one must usually pass seven such terraces, each of them of a different color, probably in accord with the alchemic principle of the interdependence of specific colors, planets, and metals. That cheerful contrast of steps and terraces goes to the very top. On the topmost ridge rises a building, the mantra of the whole ziggurat. This is a temple of no great size, or an observatory.

All these giant playthings, the Sumerian and Babylonian ziggurats, the *intihuatane* of the Incas, the Pyramids and Stonehenge, are measuring devices which function in four dimensions; in three that are exiled and in a fourth that endlessly returns home. The measurements of their angles, their slopes, and their extensions, the number of their stairways or stories, and their interdependence coincide with the cosmic chronology of our Kalpas.* Certainly a more perfect device

* Astronomy was a part of astrology. It didn't "develop" from it but was left to later generations as its most comprehensible part. Astronomy was a discipline within a wider, philosophical knowledge of the stars.

than I have ever imagined, the most beautiful snare for the great vultures of time.

I wandered for long over the scorched hillocks. They ground under my feet in a reddish foam of old sherds. The millions of potsherds on the hillocks stood out like blood-stained sweat; below them there must be something living, something huge and seized by cramps. Therefore the heat gushes out from below and not from above; from the un-excavated bedrooms, bathhouses, and guest rooms; from the streets which don't know that they are dead and wander through the skull of the Titan Ur like persistent memories. Clearly the dead don't know that they are dead and the living believe that they are alive; between them there is only one *udjat*, one brotherly eye, with which no one can any longer see. And so: strong and deep oblivion divides the living from the dead, as the Nile divides Egypt.

At long last, stunned by all this inarticulate force, I squatted in the shade thrown by the mighty flank of the ziggurat. Thus the guiding thread feels when it reaches its end; impotent to bind anything, to unite with anything. In vain is it unraveled, in vain disentangled from the red weave on which Ariadne embroidered the pattern of the Labyrinth.

In the greatest of all scars the knife now turns, turns slowly like a drowning man in an eddy. It's impossible to die or to be born to my vain perception; only some vague déjà vu infuriates me along these ways through Chaldea and Egypt.

The Sumerian watchers of the stars knew how to reckon the movements of heavenly bodies with fantastic accuracy; today, even at school, they teach that the Sumerians reckoned the orbit of the moon at only 0.4 seconds less than the scientists of Palomar and Jodrell Bank. It's not so well known that they were aware of the moons of Mars, of the speed of their movement and their distance from the mother planet—facts that have been successfully confirmed only by the most up-to-date instruments. There you are, it is the Sumerian astronomical knowledge that excites our wonder. We haven't yet even begun to marvel at their astrological knowledge, which was preserved on the summits of the ziggurats.

Can one see from here any better than from the observatory towers of the Upper City of Zagreb? Why all this game of hide-and-seek, exile and return, dream and reality? There you are, I've banished myself into the semblance of a god, immensely far, in the heavens, in the depths of the earth, in a love that doesn't exist. I allowed that god to become strong and arrogant in his belief in himself, to whip me through the world to collect evidence for him. I allowed this because it is easier to walk than to be still, and therefore I, cowardly, agreed that He lies outside myself and that He keeps me busy by His incomprehensible will.

In truth, it is easier so; in one country to write *tabule smaragdine* and in another country to decipher them with much suffering. It is easier to stride across the desert to the holy meteorite than to dig it out of one's own back garden. It is easy to wander through the world by weary ways, but it is hard to lower onself down the craters of its volcanoes, down the numbed nerves and through the curdled corridors of the blood, all the way to its white-hot beginnings, to the time when this chill planet prepared with ardor for the first man, for that one who did not come, even though he conceived all my peoples, all my Sumerians, my Egyptians, my Indians, and those I suckle and prepare for myself on the plateaus of the Cordilleras.

Can one see from here better than from the Zagreb observatory? Yes, though it is equally impossible to see; all those strong and those more humble soul gazers are equally blind in my eyes. For soul is illuminated by soul and all else is darkness.

CONCLUSION ABOUT DISTANCES

Before I constructed my own stargazing platforms and all the ziggurats, the Pyramids, the stupas, the *intihuatane*, all the measurements and snares for starry sounds and shades, before I set up the calendars of the sky and all the stars—I was myself the sky and all the stars.

Before the grapes ripened, before the wine had matured, I was drunk, dead drunk. Ah, drunkenness is older than the vine! And when I awoke from stupor, I went out to plant vineyards, to chisel jars in jasper and alabaster. And for long, long, it didn't occur to me that the vineyard and the hangover are only syllables of drunkenness. As the rose is the password for perfume, so Baghdad and Cairo and Belgrade and Zagreb and Dubrovnik are magnetic symbols which attract and collect the thoughts that I banish from myself.

Before the grapes ripened, before the wine fermented, I was drunk. Before I fell asleep and dreamed that I was awake, I was awake.

I was awake and now I dream that I am awake.

THE EGYPTIAN SCHOOL OF DEATH

The mystery reserves itself, the mystery reveals itself.

Every civilization discovers its own characteristic attitude toward death. Ancient Egypt is one of the most remarkable of them. Nowhere has that domain on the far side of the grave been developed so carefully and with more meticulous detail.* With the same pedantry and sense of realism and meticulous measure that had made it possible to erect architectural colossi, the Egyptians conducted their research into that vision of uncertain outlines: the Land of the Farther Shore.

The ancient Egyptian Land of the Farther Shore was as painstakingly parceled out and well ordered as the domain of the living. The ancient Egyptian Land of the Farther Shore

* Other than, perhaps, the insufficiently studied Andean and Yucatan civilizations and the even less known civilization of Tibet.

132

had its own divisions, its own marked-out method of settle-
ment, in short—the pillars of its existence. The ancient Egyptian Land of the Farther Shore was a specter of the dark light.

When an ancient Egyptian died, each one of all the countless beings which survived him demanded his vital share.
From the body, as if from some unsealed magic bottle, flew
out imprisoned beings, the *ka* and the *ku*, parts of its humanity, even the *ren* (name) and the *kaibit* (shadow). For
man is a family of similar but not identical beings who live
within him more or less in concord, more or less in discord.
Three thousand years in the Nile valley patiently confirmed
which of all these parts made up a man and what were the
levels of their existence.*

* Within the *kat*, the body, lives its double, the *ka*; there is also, at
the same time, the *ba*, the "soul of the heart," which has taken up its
nesting place in the heart, in the center of consciousness; there is,
furthermore, the *ren*, or the identity, and the *sahu*, the spiritual body
in which resides the immortal soul, or *ku*.

The *kat* is the part most subject to decomposition; it is able, however,
to be preserved by the special arts of embalming. All Egyptian corpses
were mummified, for the *kat* is the nest to which the double, the *ka*,
the *eidolon*, of a man most willingly returns. By its wishes and its
memories the *ka* is linked to this world and loves to play with the
things with which the *kat* played in its lifetime; it adorns itself and
clothes itself in the grave, eats and drinks, enters into the mummified
kat or, if this does not exist, into a statue of the deceased. The *ka*, obviously, is not immortal; it is only a prolonged existence, the fading of
a color in infrared distance, invisible to the naked eye. In the tomb
frescoes picturing birth, we see that man comes into the world as a
visible *kat* and as the *kat's* etheric double, the *ka*. The *ka* is what the
people of all times have called the soul of the deceased; the image of
the dead man as if printed on mist, on a substance more ethereal and
more lasting than the flesh. The *ka* separates itself from the *kat* when
a man sleeps or while he is in an unconscious state.

The part called *ba*, the "soul of the heart," is freed from the need to
repeat the game of life as played by the *ka*. On the evidence of surviving inscriptions it is not clear where the *ba* really resides; in the
tomb or in the skies. Or equally and contemporaneously in both? For
there are contradictory assertions about this.

133

For man is a swarm of many entities; a swarm that rages around some shining, quiet place. Man is a flock that flies around an unknown obelisk with a nest on its summit.

All great archaic civilizations, studying the regions of death, have arrived at similar revelations. Whoever reads the old Egyptian Book of the Dead (or, rather, the Book of Entry into the New Day) and the Tibetan *Bardo Thödol*

The *ba* holds court in the heart, which is called *ab*. Therefore the *ba* is represented as a bird with a human head, and the *ab* as its nest. On the day of judgment before Osiris, a man's heart, or *ab*, becomes counsel for the defense, or even prosecutor. *Ab* corresponds approximately to our conception of conscience. Placed on the scales of incorruptible balance, the heart reveals whether good or evil predominates in the man. If evil predominates, only then is he threatened with real death, total annihilation of his being. In a fragment from the Book of the Dead (Chapter 27) it can clearly be seen that the *ba* is an abstract conception: "O Thou [it is Orisis who is in question] who snatches the heart, who forms man's heart from his deeds even when a man does not suspect it!"

Then, too, there is the name, or *ren*, the magic key to identity. On the day of judgment, the beings call the roll; whosoever's name is lost, his being, too, is lost. The name is the reflection of the soul, never merely a chance addition to a man, but a resounding formula of man's essence. *Ren* is the secret name, the real name; as well as the *ren* every Egyptian had also his "little name," that is his false name, in order to trick enchanters and evil-intentioned sorcerers. Therefore the ceremony of christening a child was held in secret.

Sahu is the shining husk, the spiritual body for the divine and immortal soul, the *ku*. The *ku* is represented as an ibis. Esoteric Christians spoke of a "body of glory" in which the soul ascends to heaven. And the *ku*, therefore, is that seventh, diamond, part, identical with the sun's disk.

As well as those enumerated, there exist also some other components of a man's being, but these are clearly variants and aspects of the basic elements. The funeral texts mention a man's *sekhem*, in the sense of his ambition. Interesting, too, is the conception of *kaibit* (shadow), which answers completely to the modern psychoanalytic conception of that part of the personality in which are repressed instinctive desires and destructive impulses. Jung's school of analysis also refers to that part of a man's personality as his shadow.

will see that the contours of the two Lands of the Farther Shore curiously coincide. In my left hand is one, in my right hand another guidebook for the dead, two banks of the same vision, of a vision that is the same from the Himalayan peaks to the Egyptian plains.*

What reciprocity exists among all these parts of man? Do they know of one another, are they in some cause-and-effect relationship, do they exist contemporaneously or successively? What happens to the inextinguishable and immortal *ku* when the judges of the underworld hand over a man to the monster of annihilation? Ah, all that is a question on the level of the *kat*. Of that we can only feel a foreboding; only the totality of a man will perceive the totality of the world: when the eye of all six beings opens and when it sees with the precious seventh sight.

* Both the Tibetan (Mahayana) and the ancient Egyptian primers for the dead say that the dead do not know that they are "dead" and that they must first of all be convinced of this, that is to say they must be prepared for all stages in their new region of existence. Both one and the other unwearyingly draw the attention of the deceased to the possibility of advancement in the new world, and equally to the dangers of such a journey. Swedenborg, too, asserts this (*De Coelo*, ed. 1868, pp. 493-7) and even European and American spiritualists.

The second essential similarity which astounded me was the thought, already referred to, that the human being is divided into many sub-beings, alternatively, forms of reality. Taken to its conclusion, this conception looks on man as a grandiose evolution of consciousness, made up of a series of stages: every stage corresponds to a definite part of a man's being. The world in which the *ka* lives is different from the world in which the *ku* lives, as the conception of residence in the two worlds; the *ka* exists in time, the *ku* in eternity.

What the Egyptians called *ka*, the Lamaists call *charya linga* (astral body), to which belongs the astral *ka*-universe (in Tibetan recensions this universe is described as one of the crystallizations of *paradeha* or causal body) the first phase of the *bardo* process which is called *chikay-bardo*—and the causal universe corresponding to it. Yes, man is a swarm of many entities, man is a flock which flies around the summit of the world obelisk, his nest.

Linked with the conception of division, that is to say with the many levels of the human being, is the basic thought of death in one and the other: bodily death is nothing but a transformation of consciousness.

To the reader of esoteric literature it is clear that the *ku* is nothing other than the atman, that is to say the pneuma, even the Seele in the sense in which Goethe sang of it: and what else is the logos except shakti and sophia, *Sapientia Dei* and *spiritus sancti?* And what else is tao but brahman and nous? *

These intellectual identities are too impenetrable to give us any real insight. Here are some very ancient thoughts about the creative power of the word. Both in Egypt and in India, the word, primarily as an acoustic phenomenon, stands at the beginning of the creation of the world. The sound is identifiable with the cosmic breath; the most complete is the idea about the Vedanta conception *aum,* the trinity word which is the basic vibration of the cosmos and which expresses its essence. †

In one of the ancient Egyptian cosmogonies, from the era of the builders of the Great Pyramids, the spirit which resided in the primeval waters (*nun*) †† pronounced its own

* "The tao is motionless, but nonetheless there is nothing that it does not do" (*Tao Te Ching,* XXXVII).

"Brahman, unmoving, is swifter than thought; the senses cannot attain to it; it is always in advance of them. Remaining motionless, it overtakes those that rush" (*Isha Upanishad*).

"Nous is boundless and its own ruler, unmixed, separate, sufficient unto itself" (Anaxagoras).

† "*Aum!* that eternal word is all; everything that was, everything that is and that will be, and what is beyond that in eternity. Everything is *aum*" (*Mandukya Upanishad*). In the trinity word *aum,* *a* represents the beginning, *u* the transition, and *m* the end of the world.

†† In the Brahmanist cosmogonies, at the beginning of every world cycle, stand the dead, formless waters in which sleep "the germs of life" and on the face of these waters will later burst into flower Brahma, the lotus of existence.

And *nun* (in Coptic *nujn*, with the same meaning: a watery abyss) also contains in itself the dormant seeds of life. In the Heliopolitan cosmogony, the most poetic of all, the huge lotus breaks into flower on the surface of the *nun*: that lotus is the cradle of the sun on the first morning of the world and the most beautiful child, Nefer-tum, name, and that act transformed it into the image of God. The conception of the divine word is among the most ancient in Egypt: what has been uttered, that becomes. One of the most legitimate successors of ancient Egyptian spiritual maturity is the evangelist John, particularly in the first chapter of his gospel, where he speaks of the Word. Belief in the power of sound in itself is shown by the fragments of purely acoustic values that are sung in Mithraic and Gnostic liturgies.

Because of that and similar powers the word-sound is the base of magic rituals. The Brahmanist mantra is one of the weapons of high magic. The mantra is a composition of wisely chosen vibrations which, in the mouth of whoever correctly utters it, becomes a weapon in both the spiritual and bodily sphere. The ancient Greek theory of music—perhaps of Pelasgian origin or perhaps inherited from Egypt—teaches that knowledge of the key note of some body or object means power over that body or that object. Mantra is allied to the ancient Egyptian conception of *ren* or the secret name.* The hieroglyph r-n is a picture of a mouth above

---

awakens in its calyx. The myth of the golden babe is to be found in the oldest version of the Rig-Veda. Sometimes the *nun* is presented as the face of the original giant (Purusha, Prayapati), who with head and arms rises out of himself.

* When the cunning enchantress Izida poisoned the father of the gods with his own saliva in the form of a snake and when in his death pangs he called on her for help, she in return demanded the greatest of gifts: the father's secret name, the source of his almighty power. Obviously the Hebrew Tetragrammaton (the four-letter name of God) stems from the ancient Egyptian *ren*.

Egyptian monotheism is expressed in the well-known formula of the Hermopolitan tradition: *Ra* is he who created his own names—that is to say the other gods. The first so-named structure is the Hermopolitan ogdoad (the eight-member conclave of the gods). The ancient Egyptian name of Hermopolis is Kemeni, which means the "eight-town." The ogdoad is made up of four pairs of elements which when uttered begin to separate from the One.

the surface of the water: a picture of the creation of the world. The greater part of the Book of the Dead is a miscellany juggling with magic names. For every image "flashes" its flickering symbol, its sounding "name," and every image "responds" or "listens" to him who has its name in his possession. The initiate with knowledge of the resounding concord of reality can by correct recitation control the destinies of beings and things, in other words his own fate.

The mythology of medieval civilizations abounds in lyres and flutes* which build up and trumpets which destroy. The flutes of Osiris and of Pan, the lyres of Amphitrion and Orpheus, are examples of harmony with the rhythm of nature, whereas the trumpets of Jericho are an example of discord with that rhythm, an example, therefore, of the destructive clash of vibrations.

Even in the most superficial conversation on the spiritual similarity of mutually distinct civilizations (distant not only in space but also in time) it is impossible not to mention the man-god who by his sacrifice makes possible the world. He is *protos anthropos*, the first man Manichean and Gnostic, Adam Kadmon of the cabala, the first player in the universal tragedy. He is Purusha, the dismembered giant of the cosmos, the fragments of whose body become many-faceted reality. He also becomes Sati, whose broken body was scattered through all India; he was the Sumerian dragonlike Tiamat; he was, finally, Osiris, with all his subgroups, which sprouted up along the shores of the Mediterranean. The breaking into pieces of the original body is an omen of the first stage of the world. The ideal oneness disintegrates into imperfect and painful multiplicity. Yes, in all visions of the transition from chaos to cosmos, at that very transition, stands One Image, that transition is itself One Image. It is a symbol

* Like Krishna, Osiris enchanted his listeners with the magic sounds of his flute. The legend of Osiris says that the founder of Egyptian civilization tamed the half-savage denizens of the marshes with the gentle notes of his flute.

138

of universality and bliss. And the resultant man is a fragment of a god—a part of Osiris, a part that longs to revert to the wholeness of his image. That longing for wholeness and the effort of searching for it are incorporated in Isis. Isis is the name of the basic instinct of totality and union, which is not only the characteristic trait of man, but of the whole mineral, vegetable, and animal kingdom.

The ancient Egyptian principle of the duality of the world, so akin to the Chinese conception of yang-yin is, unfortunately, only indirectly attainable, that is to say in the philosophical-scientific systems that were inspired by ancient Egyptian thought for hundreds of years after the ancient Egyptian civilization had ceased to exist creatively. (At first it seems that a wonderful abundance of the works of that civilization remains, an abundance more numerous than the remains of any other civilization. However, of its spiritual culture, of written evidence, comparatively little survives. The most important remains of ancient Egyptian ideology are funeral inscriptions on the walls of tombs, epitaphs on sarcophagi, and comments on papyri which accompany mummified travelers into the Land of the Farther Shore. But in relation to the total of three thousand years of vigorous culture, these are pitiful fragments. Of the greatest mathematicians of the Mediterranean region only one papyrus, unique but imperfect, with illustrated instructions has been preserved. We call it Pythagorean, but it was known in Egypt for hundreds of years before Pythagoras. The greatest builders in the world have not handed down to us descriptions of their methods of construction and engineering; therefore their methods have remained a secret to the present day. There are no detailed medical, astrological, grammatical, or philosophical texts, nor are there manuscripts of poetical works or of the mythological dramas that were performed in the sanctuaries of the temples. Why has no anthology, similar to that at Nippur, been excavated on Egyptian soil, or a library like that of Assurbanipal? Where is that legendary

Book of Books of Thoth, of which Clement of Alexandria writes and which Iamblichus asserts that he saw and that it consisted of forty-two volumes in which were contained all the knowledge and all the wisdom possible to man? Where are the papyri from the great library at Kemeni and where are those from the treasury at Om, the oldest and the greatest ancient Egyptian seat of learning? But wait a moment! An easy answer is at hand; everything was consumed in the flames of the great fire at Alexandria; the precious rolls of papyri flared for months in the furnaces of the Arab hammams. Whoever accepts that as the answer should not accept it as the whole answer. For that means casting doubt on the keepers of the treasuries, on the Egyptian *hiereoi* who jealously preserved the esoteric nucleus of Egypt from any contact with the uninstructed. In the time of the final breakdown of a civilization that seemed to be eternal, perhaps they deliberately destroyed the written sacred things.)

But in this case the question is irrelevant. Our aim is to trace ancient Egyptian principle in later Greek and early Christian pictures of the world and especially in the occult doctrine of alchemy. In all probability alchemy is the only direct inheritance of ancient Egyptian dialectic thought. The medieval mystical practitioners recognized world conflicts in chemical elements (sulphur and quicksilver); and the whole tangled and long-lasting *opus operatum* (Arabic: *amal*) was undertaken because of the final mystical marriage (*conniunctio oppositorum*) and because of the *filius* (*lapis*). *Opus* was understood as a true parallel to the spiritual unwinding in the searcher himself; *opus* was a reflection of the intangible on the tangible, the abstract process materialized. Furthermore, all that painful lingering over retorts also served to veil the real motives of alchemy, a means of concealment both from public opinion and from its still-unqualified disciples. *Opus* was an effective defense against naïve and unworthy minds such as surrounded the ranks of the alchemists. For as long as they were satisfied with laboratory practice and its prosaic aim, gold, only the closed, enlightened circle of alchemists knew that *aurum nostrum non est aurum vulgi.*

If we consider the few surviving fragments of ancient Egyptian "proto-alchemic" reasoning (amongst which the most important is the *Tabula Smaragdina,* an Arabic transcript of an Egyptian master to his pupils, Hermes-Thoth) we see only the ignoble outline of the dialectical thinking of the ancient Egyptian intellectual elite. For the Indians as well this was only the first stage of reasoning. The most exalted zenith of the ancient Egyptian philosophers was on the poetic horizon of insight, and from it can be seen that contradictions were not "abolished" or "reconciled" but never even existed.* There has always existed only That One (*tad ekam* for the Vedantic sages, "the miracle of Oneness" for Hermes, and the "Kingdom of Heaven" for Jesus and his

---

* "Truth above truths, the most true, without falsehood. As it is higher, so is it lower. As below, so is it above. We must achieve that marvel of Oneness. All that is created is created by mind deeply penetrating Oneness. . . . Everything wonderful is born there and its power is supreme. Throw it on the earth and the earth will separate from the fire. The intangible is set apart from the tangible. . . . It ascends to the heavens and again descends to earth, linking the powers above with the powers below. . . . By it the world came to pass. That is the way by which, in the future, many wonders will be revealed.

"I am Hermes, the threefold sage, so called because I hold in my hands the three principles of universal wisdom.

"Thus ends the revelation according to the sun" (*Tabula Smaragdina,* L. Menard's version).

The human spirit cannot escape certain experiences. They always repeat themselves, identically, not because tradition renews them but because they are inborn in man's spiritual constitution. As he was dying on the cross, St. Paul sang from the same heights of perception as Hermes. At his own request he was crucified head downward so that, in that position, he symbolized the final identity of that which is above and that which is below, that which is to the right and that which is to the left. For in that position the right side hangs and the left is upright or vice versa, as Paul's words about martyrdom clearly confirm:

"O name of the cross, thou hidden mystery! . . . I seize thee now, I that am at the end of my delivery hence (or, of my coming hither). . . . Unless ye make the things of the right hand as those of the left,

141

early followers). Their conflicts and their mutual dynasties fall, therefore, into the world of chimeras and searches in the involvement with the *opus*, that is to say in the world of *maya* and *lila*.

That "miracle of Oneness," created by basic human meditation on reality, leads us from far, in all directions. Some think that the miracle of Oneness can be explained only by extraterrestrial intervention, which is, obviously, much less miraculous than that similar key visions should have appeared spontaneously in the human soul, without regard to external differences, that is to historical, geographic, climatic, and other factors.

I return now to the theme that drove me to set out on this path into the wilderness. That theme was the Egyptian Schools. I call them schools of death, despite the fact that they should have been given the completely opposite name, and that there are certain indications that they were, in fact, really so named, that is to say "Schools of Life." The conception "death" is, moreover, responsible for several misunderstandings. But even so it affords us occasion for agreement which, even if only partially established, enriches us more than any possible misunderstandings could deprive us. The meditative-emotional connotations linked with the idea of death in the interpretations of orthodox Christianity and materialism are very few and vague. Here there is a possibility that our own poor orchestration of this essential concept may be enriched by a few very outstanding tones.

What we understand as death the Egyptians conceived as one of the possibilities on the ladder of postbodily forms of life. Death annihilation and death dream are stages of the Egyptian underworld pyramid: annihilation is only one of the fates that can happen to a man in the Duat state, and

---

and those of the left as those of the right, and those that are above as those below, and those that are behind as those that are before, ye shall not have knowledge of the kingdom" (*The Apocryphal New Testament*, ed. M. R. James, Oxford, 1924, pp. 334 and 335).

the Christian death dream (till the Judgment Day) also has its place in the Egyptian labyrinth, but the path that leads toward the way out of that labyrinth—the leitmotif—into the "light of the New Day" is a wakeful, calm transformation of the human soul into the divine universal spirit. To die was, for the Egyptians, an imperfective verb; as the living live so do the dead live a dead life and as life is an art so, too, death is an art. An art that can be learned. Therefore there were schools.

Indeed, despite so many esoteric schools and countless self-styled gurus, the Oriental man must settle the question of life-death for himself; no one else and nothing else can solve it in his stead. The path to understanding is the path to God, a strictly individual effort, and therefore in the Orient there are no intermediate bodies such as the Christian church —an organization that performs a great part of the task instead of us. For no one can grant a man eternal life except himself.

As for the schools, they taught the procedure of composure: that is to say they exercised their pupils in the achievement of that spiritual-bodily condition which is *conditio sine qua non* of higher understanding. It was a scientific technique, worked out to the minutest detail. There are countless such techniques in the East, but the aim is always and everywhere the same: how to reach that superconscious part of oneself which unites us with the cosmic consciousness, how to attain "the miracle of Oneness," to travel to the heavenly kingdom. The majority of such schools were hermetic —in other words the teaching was a jealously preserved secret handed down only to the chosen and only by word of mouth.* And what was written was written in symbols which later, uninstructed generations accepted and interpreted lit-

* "The Egyptians preserved the secret of their mysteries and did not defile their understanding of divine things by confiding them to the ears of the unworthy: they preserved them for the heir to the throne and for those priests who had distinguished themselves for virtue and wisdom" (Clement of Alexandria).

143

erally, never penetrating into the core of their philosophies.*

One of the most impenetrable institutions of ancient times was the Egyptian temple school. The priests of Busiris, On, Sais, Karnak, Bubastis, Hermopolis, Herakliopolis, and Memphis were not half-persons like Hamlet. They did not employ a Horatio to tell at least half of their story. In their case, all was silence. A vow of silence was demanded of every pupil about everything that in the course of their schooling they saw and learned.† They were enveloped in absolute silence, like a mummy in its wrappings.

---

* One of these philosophical systems of signs and symbols was the Egyptian picture writing, that is to say a written form. These signs and symbols the literate and the initiated used as cyphers of communication, whereas for the uninitiated the symbols continued to have their conventional meaning. That old pedant Herodotus, who, measuring-staff in hand, traveled around the Mediterranean, bears witness to this. What is important is that Herodotus attended the school of the temple at On, that same school where Moses and Akhenaten studied, that same school which, probably, Pythagoras, Plato, and Plutarch attended. (It is perfectly evident that Pythagoras at least "borrowed" his doctrine of the transmigration of souls from the Egyptians.)

We have also the evidence of the initiate Apuleius, another foreigner, who completed the first grade at the temple of the mysteries of Isis on the tiny island of Philae; and of the Syrian Iamblichus, the Greeks Stobaeus, Proclus, Diodorus, and Plutarch. Plotinus, too, bears witness to the Egyptian picture writing and confirms that that writing was made up of several layers of interpretation. What was shown to the literates and what the picture writing meant was accessible to clerks and other lay experts; what, however, the letter pictures *concealed* was accessible only to the initiates.

† This went so far that Herodotus refrains from even recording the name of Osiris (or Isis) in his description of the mysteries in *Euterpe,* his travel book on Egypt. Instead, he says: "a god whose name a religious scruple forbids me from mentioning" (*Euterpe,* 61) and: "of these mysteries which I personally got to know I do not wish to say a word, for I am bound by reverent silence" (*Euterpe*).

Otherwise he writes in great detail about everday customs, descriptions of buildings, and the natural and historical features of the country. That is why his conscious restraint is most striking whenever

But silence is not exclusively an ancient Egyptian quality. It is the defensive stockade around all ancient and contemporary ashrams. For knowledge is a mortal danger and can be charged with a destructive power if it be defiled by covetous and unilluminated souls. The more noble the initial

---

in the course of a detailed description he approaches the forbidden subject.

This inhibition sounds childish and affected, the fruit of Egypt's decadence (fifth century B.C.). The names of Osiris and Isis had been on everyone's lips for two or three thousand years! This formalistic insistence bears witness to the moribund disintegration of Egyptian spiritual leadership. The real mystery preserves itself, even as it reveals itself.

Apuleius is infinitely more thorough in his report of his own initiation in the temple of Isis:

"Probably, eager reader, you are burning with desire to find out what took place there, what was pronounced there. I would tell you, were I permitted to do so and you would learn were it intended that you should learn. But both my tongue and your ears would be drenched in sin should I hasten to satisfy such idle curiosity. Yet perhaps you are moved by pious yearning, so I will no longer keep you in torment. Listen then, and believe, for what I have to tell you is the truth.

"I approached the precincts of death, I stepped on the threshold of Proserpine. I was blown through the elements and was once again restored to earth. I saw the sun shining with full force at midnight, I drew near to the greater gods and to the gods of the underworld and made obeisance to them" (*Metamorphoses*, XI).

The experience described by the garrulous Apuleius was samadhi, the indescribable core of all mystical states. Its first characteristic is the revocation of the limitations of space and time. The samadhi state of mind is the wheel on which are wiped out the three greatest and most convincing of illusions: space, time, and causality.

Herodotus's total and Apuleius's partial discipline of silence is not so eloquent as that ancient Egyptian prayer to Thoth, the eye of wisdom:

"O Thoth, thou sweet water-spring for the thirsty in the desert! Thou water, hidden to him who calls for you in words and revealed to him who searches for you with silence. Whoso is silent you will help and whoso speaks you will leave parching" (according to Wallis Budge).

thought the more cynically it is abused by scoundrels. Furthermore, knowledge of this sort will be of harm to him who is unprepared to penetrate it, even as poison will harm an untrained body. The ancient Egyptian *Hiereoi* knew that truth would not bring enlightenment if we hear it at an unsuitable moment, that is to say at a time when we are not sufficiently mature. In fact, at such a time it will confuse or even repel us. The mysterious words of one of the greatest gurus (Jesus the Jew) are clear in the framework of this ancient thought: "Whoso is near me is near the fire"—truth, this time incarnate in man, is like a fire. It can warm but can also consume.

Every hermetic society, in order to preserve the secrecy of its teaching, has its own password and its own private language. Or, if it has not such a language, it has a secret key for reading otherwise commonplace letters, words, and meanings. The Sufi school makes use of a numerical system which replaces the alphabet and which corresponds to a specific arrangement of ideas. In that new arrangement of ideas poetic image or even suggestive sound plays the role of a specialized term. The Krishna mystics wrote the most sensual lyrics, for they recognized bodily ecstasy as the sole suitable allusion to spiritual ecstasy. Also, when the medieval or contemporary Sufi makes use of the Osirian expressions "death" and "resurrection" he understands them as processes that involve *nafs*, consciousness. The alchemists made use of a whole "forest of symbols" from mythology and metallurgy to remind them of the states of consciousness through which the seeker after truth passes.

The language of esoteric learning is a poetical language: a language within a language, made up of ordinary words which by the use of a special key are given another, deeper, significance. In the Buddhist tale of the girl Kisha Gotama it is, above all, a magic landscape that is described: under Kisha's glance a pile of ashes becomes a pile of precious stones. The allegory is that the gaze of the inspired turns every day into a holiday, the prosaic word into poetry.

146

As today, so in times past: myths and stories can be read on various levels. The first level is simple, the literal meaning of the tale; the next step is a fragmentary insight into a deeper reality—it seems that the tale in some instances plunges into that reality; the third and last level is full comprehension of the metaphysical content of the tale (or of some abstract symbol). The basic layers recognized in the body of the myth are really the basic layers and forms of the reader's consciousness.

As in times past, so, too, today. For in the most common forms of consciousness myths are only fables that at their best enclose in themselves fundamental emotional idioms. For the rarest type of consciousness, however, myth—and all accomplishments of symbolic reality, that is to say every form of art—is an a-b-c of a higher order.

Whenever I wander through Egyptian time, I inquire about the drama of the soul told about the divine pentagram Osiris-Isis-Set-Nephthys-Horus.* Most often my comrades on

---

* Plutarch's *De Iside et de Osiride* is clearly the lastest and the simplest version of the myth. But that is the only "biography" of Egyptian gods that has been preserved from beginning to end. In the hagiographical and magic papyri are scattered fragments of the same legend. A comparison between Plutarch's report and the Egyptian fragments shows that in essentials the fables coincide.

Osiris is a good king, who is treacherously killed by his evil brother Set. His body is nailed into a coffin and cast into the Nile. His woebegone queen, Isis, sets out to find the coffin and after many wanderings arrives at Byblos, where the coffin has become entangled in a tamarisk root and has grown into its trunk. Serving in the household of the king of Byblos as the wet nurse of his son, Isis eventually receives a reward for her miraculous service: the right to split the holy tree, which the king has in the meantime used as a supporting pillar of the palace. Isis returns with the coffin to Egypt. By her enchantments she manages to breathe life into Osiris's corpse. In the ritual of resurrection she is assisted by her sister Nephthys, well versed in death. (According to one version Isis conceives Horus by the dead Osiris.) But Set finds and once again kills the king, dismembers his body, and scatters the pieces over the whole land of Egypt. The faithful Isis sets out again in search of the pieces. Wherever she finds some part of

Osiris's corpse she buries it and sets up a shrine. Flying with the child Horus from her persecutor Set, she arrives at an enchanted island which floats upon the Nile. There she leaves Horus in the care of the enchantress of the island and herself wanders on through the wilderness of Egypt until she finds the last piece (in another version, the last piece, the phallus, is never found, for it has been swallowed by a Nile fish; hence the religious ban on eating fish). In the end Osiris is again resurrected by the aid of his divine father Ra and goes to live and to judge in the Land of the Farther Shore. In the meantime Horus has grown up and become an avenger. He goes into battle against his uncle (the dialogue of Horus with the dead Osiris is the prototype of every later intimate conversation of this kind, of which, naturally, the most supreme example is Hamlet's midnight conversation with his murdered father). After a long and complicated struggle Horus is victorious (several versions exist about the outcome of the struggle; one of them tells that Horus does not kill Set but only drives him out of the land, another that Horus mutilates—castrates—his uncle and, according to a third version, the gods divide the kingdom between Horus and Set).

Obviously, there are several variants of the same myth. Some are themes perhaps linked with a specific historical character (with the first unifier of Egypt), and others even with the matriarchal cult of the Great Mother. But the origin of the legend is far less interesting than the metaphysical inevitability that has become expressed in it. The interpreters of that were the nameless thinkers, the originators of Egyptian civilization.

In the drama two basic principles, incarnate in twin brothers, are pitted against one another. One is wicked and the other good. (The same paradox of relatives in conflict is to be found in Sumerian, Greek, and Nordic mythology. The Sumerian queen of heaven and light, Inanna, has a twin sister, Ereshkigal, who rules over darkness and the underworld. There is a similar relationship between Zeus and Hades [originally a god], between Baldur and Hoder, and, inspired by that, the stories of Jacob and Esau and of Romulus and Remus.) One of the oldest and deepest of human presentiments is that suspicion that evil and good are two correlating forces of a single reality. Or, "to speak in the Indian manner," that one unique being divides within himself his higher and his lower nature and that partition, that conflict, makes possible the dynamism of the world.

Osiris is a good Set, Set is an evil Osiris. That identity of opposites is taken still farther in the wives of the brothers, Isis and Nephthys. They also are twins; one is the embodiment of the life force (Isis), whereas the other commands the regions of death (Nephthys). But not only are Isis and Nephthys doubles, they are also the sisters of their husbands. These relationships, at once simple and complicated, create four points mutually equidistant and opposed in pairs and also individually. The first sketch of that relationship is a square.

But there is a suspicion that within this game there were also diagonal relationships, for Nephthys was for a time the wife of Osiris (the king was married automatically to the sisters of his wife) and by him she conceived Anubis, the black jackal, the guide of souls into the underworld. That devoted seeker of the Great Muse, Robert Graves, suggests that Isis was in secret accord with the murderer of her husband. Thus one obtains a rectangle with two transversals; to each side of the rectangle belongs an equilateral triangle.

If we delve still deeper into this arsenal of symbols we shall find that a triangle means a trinity, or a three-member godhead. Most of the Egyptian cities were ruled by such a trinity: father-mother-son. The Theban trinity comprised Ammon, his wife, Nut, and his son Konsu; the Heliopolitan was Ptah-Sekhmet-Nefertum.

Such a complex image recalls a *yantra*, the composition of which is also strictly mathematical. The protagonists of the myth are arranged like the set points of a geometric image. Careful consideration of that image irresistibly reminds us of a pyramid.

Let us take a further look: as well as those four correlated images a fifth appears in the story—Horus, who resolves the dramatic denouement and puts things in their places. Horus is the outcome of all the indicated relationships, and although he is in fact Isis's son, everyone in his or her own way has contributed to his birth. Horus is the fifth element, the sum of the two pairs. The fifth member is a way out into a fifth dimension, into height; geometrically speaking, Horus is the point at which meet and vanish all the lines of the rectangular base. So is derived the pyramid.

In man's presentation the rectangle has always represented external space, the four quarters of the world; the triangle symbolizes the inner world (Plato also says that the ternary principle is linked with the idea and the quaternary with the achievement of that idea). The five-member drama, whose total expression is the pyramid, is a memorial to the unity of the triangle and the rectangle, the world and man. The pyramid portrays total reality.

To many this mathematical rule may seem precipitate or hazardous and the metaphysical content implied by it only an irresponsible play of thought, whether in ancient Egypt or in modern speculation. But no one is forced to accept such an interpretation of the myth. The these paths are the archeologists. Some are very passionate and very clairvoyant pryers; in other words, there are some amongst them who can "sniff out" where some greater or lesser bone of a buried giant may be unearthed. But the majority of them squat patiently around holes in the ground recording and classifying the fragments that emerge into the sunlight.

No, they cry in answer, Osiris is in no way a symbol of spiritual experience; he personifies the green valley of the Nile, and nothing more! Then they talk to me of Attis-Tammuz-Zagreus-Orpheus, of the martyrdom of the goddess's son. Sometimes they even mention Baldur, sometimes even Prajapati, practically never our Slav Jarilo. That was a plowman's psyche, they keep repeating, obsessed by the death and rebirth of vegetation. That was the psyche which created the myth of Osiris-Tammuz-Zagreus. That myth, therefore, reflected the "plowman's" reality. That is all. And there, where they should really begin, the majority of interpretations stop. In truth, the mystery reserves itself, the mystery reveals itself.

It is certain that Osiris-Tammuz-Zagreus is greenness personified; certainly it is a unity that exists thanks to that greenness. And just because it is greenness personified, soaked in the life-giving substance, it is useful as a name for

---

first, symbolic, transfer of the crude fable takes place on the level of natural forces; on this level Osiris and Set represent the Nile and the desert. I have nothing against such an interpretation. But it is not all-embracing; it goes no farther than the world of appearances, which for the Egyptian thinkers, lovers of abstraction, is far too low a target.

Let us examine once more those strange relationships within the drama. The basic rivals are Osiris and Set, twins. Isis and Nephthys may be regarded as their two functions, two emanations. They act between the brothers, constantly passing from light into darkness, from hatred to love, and back again. Twin sisters, wives of twin brothers, their twin widows. A structure simple and delicate, reminiscent of the tarot structure, for it rests on the mystic harmony of numbers.

an inexplicable idea. That idea would be far less suitably designated by an expression, let us say "resurrection." The ancient Egyptian philosophers did not create the Osiris myth; they adapted it from the people's tradition and perhaps, to a certain extent, modified it, just as the Buddhist and Christian teachers did with the pagan tales and myths.

From the very earliest times there was a twofold understanding of Osiris. For the majority Osiris was the name of the greenness; for the minority the greenness itself was *only a particular name*, that is to say one of the names of an inexplicable reality. The whole universe was a huge papyrus leaf inscribed with name symbols of that reality.*

* We find the most condensed expression of that understanding in the legendary Hermes-Thoth:

"Look at this sky and its stars and lights and clouds, look at this land and its mountains, rivers and plants. All that is naught else than the image of the divine will; and the totality of the universe is a world picture, a manuscript, a giant papyrus scroll written by the hand of God. Strive therefore to read and to understand this open book offered to you also, this revelation of almighty power" (Hermes Trismegistus, L. Ménard version).

This view of the world is as old as Egyptian civilization itself. The oldest inscriptions known to us are those from the tombs in the pyramid of King Unas (fifth dynasty, roughly 2500 B.C.). These aspects of the regions on the Farther Shore are so bright and strong that they give the impression of a hallucination. But despite that "psychedelic" quality these inscriptions are crystal clear as a picture of that world:

> You are devoted to your mother Nut
> in the Coffin—her name;
> She embraces you in the Sarcophagus, her name,
> and you approach her in the Tomb, her name.
>
> Pyramid texts, 616

Indeed, the more we ascend into the past, the more unreal are the powers that inhabit human space, the more real the man who lives in the invisible world. The visible is more and more lost in the invisible. And man ever more easily sees himself a part of the enormous totality of the cosmos. "Atum is the god that completes every man!"

151

Is the marrow of this teaching represented by the ankh symbol, the symbol of eternal life? I believe that there is an allusion to this in the final secret of the famous Osirian mysteries; to the mystery of resurrection, to the eternal rising of Osiris from the illusion of death.*

The Egyptian architects, too, confirm this, in their own way. Whatever is older is more abstract in outline, more devoted to monumentality and simplicity. It seems to us that it was impossible for such simplicity not to pay heed to its predecessors with bitter experience in unnecessary complexity. But nowhere is there a trace of imperfection or uncertainty: the purest lines are the most ancient; the façade of Zoser's composition of buildings is most restrainedly devoid of everything that is not essential. They stand at the very beginning of Egyptian civilization like a great question mark. Is it possible to achieve such a level of simplicity, functional and aesthetic, without long and painstaking development? Yet there are no traces of such a development, nor any answer to the previous question. The fact is that Egyptian art is at its most perfect in its official beginning.

* The mysteries (Egyptian *shesh-tau*) were moralities held in the naos of the temple, or in an inner court, or, more rarely, in separate chapels which were called Osiris's shrines. The *shesh-tau* were pantomime musical dramatic spectacles, certainly the first in the world featuring a divine death and resurrection, in fact the first masses. This is what Iamblichus, the pupil of Plotinus, has to say of them:

"The performance has, indeed, a sacramental meaning inexpressible in words. . . . It is a perfect, faultless performance, a sublime play of symbols whose irresistible power makes it possible for the mind to comprehend the divine" (*De mysteriis,* I, II).

According to Plutarch, Isis herself established the mysteries as a memorial to her own and Osiris's sufferings and to bring solace to all who are enlightened.

The transcript of the priest Iger-Nefert from the time of the XIIth dynasty has been preserved. The priest describes the flow and appearance of the holy day at Abydos (the straightening of Osiris's tree, the *dyed*). He, naturally, describes only the open and public part of the performance. For, parallel with the play, on a public stage under the open sky, another, secret, play is performed in the shrine of the temple.

Herodotus asserts that the Dionysian mysteries were brought to Greece from Egypt and that one of the enlightened, Melampus, a

No, those are fantasies, say my comrades the archeologists. Alas, nothing is more inimical to a great truth than a small one; not even a lie attacks it so bitterly.*

Like a beast to a dried-up water hole I come to Benares, to Dendera, to Thebes, to Ur and Babylon, to Delphi and Byblos, to Buddgaya and Elephanta, and to unlucky Abydos and still more unlucky Sinai. As a beast with fading hearing, I try to listen to the forces in the deep massif of the Andes. My incompleteness is such that I don't dare to know; I only suspect. Wherever I go I ask for a teacher, I search for him as a dream for its dreamer; to fulfill myself I search for him as thirst searches for water—to disappear. I am filled by its silence as a well with water; how can I drink from it?

Ah, all that is because I think of myself as a stone at the wellhead and not as living water in the depths. All that because I search so stubbornly for a Chaldean, though I know well that in the end I alone can interpret my dreams and my teachers and all the knowledge that they can bring to me. All those cities, all those images, are only hieroglyphs which my teacher—my own soul—discusses with me. Sometimes I hear, sometimes I understand.

Man is divided into six parts and the seventh part is the whole. The six parts do not know one another, the seventh is their uncomprehended unity. Six parts are subject to death,

---

Greek, established festivals in Greece which were in spirit and ritual completely Osirian. Herodotus, who was familiar with both, says that the ritual part "coincided intentionally in all its details" except for the sacrifice of a pig, for this was not practiced in Greece, and the choral dances which were not customary in Egypt.

* Truth resembles the pyramid of Imhotep, the stepped pyramid. From the lower step man rises to the higher and is never without fresh perspectives. But he who is on the lowest step does not see, and therefore does not accept, the perspective of him who is on a higher step. And he who stands on the height includes in his perspective all the perspectives beneath him. Intolerance is the mark of those who have only just begun to climb.

but the totality of them is immortal—its symbol is the sun, the precious disk.

The Egyptian school was the school of the experience of death. Certainly, the problem of death has never been resolved, but at the same time the problem of life has never been resolved. For life and death are twin sisters, Isis and Nephthys. Hermetic Egypt led its chosen ones to confirm by their own direct experience what happens when the body dies. The aim of the training was to make men recognize that they are immortal, and they got to know that by the experience of their own skins and not by theological and philosophic arguments. Few were the pupils who endured all the trials and all the traps on their way to the third level of enlightenment. The journey through the Land of the Farther Shore was made step by step, tentatively, as if one walked on a knife blade. The long-prepared consciousness led into the region of so-called death and returned once more into "life"; and every time the pupil went farther, deeper, and remained longer. Was that achieved with the aid of drugs of the mescalin type or by special exercises and breathing techniques in the manner of yoga? That we do not know and we have no information about it. But there is no reason to doubt that the Egyptian experience in this field was essentially different from the experiences of Eleusinian, Lamaist, Taoist, Hindu, and probably the Inca schools; a voluntarily achieved astral journey.*

* In the Tibetan lamaseries one of the subjects of the curriculum is *phowa. Phowa* is the power of projecting one's own consciousness into the body of another person.

Unfortunately, Europe is unskilled in such consciously directed metempsychosis and in the science of death. Only two medieval treatises exist concerning the art of dying. One is the *Ars Moriendo* and the other the *De arte Moriendi,* both by unknown authors. In its own times and in Orphic circles a handbook, *Descent into Hades,* circulated. To this meager family may be added Swedenborg's famous book *On Heaven and Hell.*

It seems that, except for ours, no other civilization saw in death the

Linked by a slender umbilical cord to man's body, the ka returns and departs the more willingly and the more simply. The goal of the priestly schools was that the chosen ones, that is to say those capable of understanding, could help the ka and the ku to free themselves at will from bodily life. Linked by this thin cord to his body, a man's ka flies out and returns, until one day the man realizes that there is no death; only grades within an enormous life. At the summit of that grandiose vertical perspective shines the jewel disk. Osiris lords it at the apex of every man. When that is known and appreciated by one's own effort and experience, then the teaching is ended, for there is nothing more to learn.

Egyptian civilization is dead, its ankh is lost. Dead is he who took his blood, tied it in a knot, and hanged it as a challenge to the unenlightened sword that carved its way from the southern Balkans to Egypt, Persia, and India.* Dead is the incomparable Hermes the Thrice-Born, though

---

cessation of human existence. This "civilization of ours" suggested here, perhaps with unpardonable nonchalance, I have wished to designate as the period that began with the industrial and technological revolution of the West and, consequently, the glorification of the rational in man. But nonetheless, more than any other, our civilization suffers from the fear of death. Death is taboo in conversation, in thought, and in deed. That central factor of our lives is skirted around, repressed, in all our conscious energy. No one today organizes the site of his death with such intimate enjoyment as the man of times past. Save for morbid eccentrics, no one any longer keeps in his house decorative urns holding the ashes of the deceased, or buries the bones of his ancestors under the threshold of his villa. For *Neobarbarus occidentalis* death is an absurdity from which one flees whenever one can. As if one's attitude toward death does not ordain one's attitude toward life!

* When Alexander, educated in the rational teaching of Aristotle, found himself faced by the subtle mystery of the East—which he conquered only externally—he, defeated in himself, cut the knot. Then the East annihilated him, it intoxicated him, it cast a spell on him, convinced him that he was the son of Ammon. He died with mind and senses disturbed, alienated from all men.

fragments of his knowledge still linger in the cabala and, alas, in the greatly simplified tarot in the hands of ignoramuses. Dead is Imhotep, the first imperial highness of knowledge. Egypt's teachers themselves announced the downfall of their caste and their learning.* As, too, the Tibetan lamas. And, like the Tibetan lamas, they knew that the men of the coming millennia will not take the path to the heights of the spirit, but will descend into the ever denser night of the world, into the kingdom of Set, into the pit of Kali-yuga.

As beasts come to shrunken springs to drink, so, too, shall we come to the cities that sway on the shoulders of sunken giants; the cities of Egypt, of India, of Mesopotamia. From below the plane of the teachers shines the completeness that liberates us from the limitations of karma; from above its incompleteness answers *for in nature man alone is incomplete; his completion expands within his spirit, which has no frontiers.*

---

* "Dost thou not know, O Thoth, that Egypt is the picture and embodiment of heaven, that the imprint of the almighty order is here on the soil of this land? But nonetheless know that a time will come when it will seem that the Egyptians honored their gods to no purpose with such devotion and that all their chanting was sterile and impotent. The divine spirit will leave the land and rise into the heavens, deserting Egypt, its ancient residence . . . and thus this land, devoted to so many altars and temples, will cover only graves and corpses. O Egypt, Egypt! Of your veneration will remain only vague, turbid tales in which those who come after will no longer believe; they will remain vain words carved in stone, witnesses to a faith that has vanished" (Hermes Trismegistus, L. Ménard version).

Of the remaining "prophetic" literature of ancient Egypt, the most impressive fragment is the account of the priest Neferrohu, an echo of which we find in the texts of the Old Testament:

"The wild beasts of the desert will drink the waters of Egypt and will be at peace, for there will be none to drive them away."

LETTER TO ABYDOS

Freedom? Isn't that service to a real master?

I have a serpent in my heart; I have had it for a long time,
Um Seti; and I would rather that I had not, or at least that
I had no heart. That serpent in my heart, Um Seti, is the
question of our proofs: yours and mine.

They say that you are mad.* But are not your proofs that

---

* Now I must tell your story, Um Seti, for without it my letter would
not be comprehensible, nor would the torment that allies me to you be
clear. For another reason also; more and more the conviction thickens
within me that poetry is inseparable from the times and the events in
which it appears; verses, texts, are only a part of a whole which happens
silently, magnificently, independently. My letter, therefore, is a part
of a whole that was begun several decades ago, when you appeared in
Egypt—or perhaps three and a half millennia ago when you also, you
and no one else, first appeared in Egypt.

Around the beginning of this century you, at that time a little
English girl, suspected for the first time that your spiritual homeland
was ancient Egypt. As you grew up, that conviction became firmer
and you were filled with inexplicable memories of the court and the
temple of the Pharaoh Seti, memories that flabbergasted the experts:
the Egyptologists and psychiatrists. For those were the memories of
one who recalled her life in all its details; someone who recalled her
life and not her dream of life.

Later came the final and decisive break with England, similar to a
suicide. For capacity for life and capacity for death are the same ca-

three or four millennia ago you were the mother of the Pharaoh Seti equally as firm as mine,* which I today dig out for my diamond Pharaoh? Proofs, my dear, proofs? The things of which we speak and those about which we keep silent are not capable of proof: they are, they are not. They are obvious or are not, so that proofs are superfluous. No one needs to prove that the sun shines when it is shining, or that it does not shine when it is not shining. Proofs are needed only when we lose our inborn direct knowledge, when we close our third eye, Um Seti, that eye which sees the world.

I have a serpent in my bosom; for a long time I have had it, and I would gladly have either a serpent or a heart. And that serpent in my bosom, Um Seti, is the question of what

---

pacity; whoever knows how to live also knows how to die. You came, therefore, to Egypt as a draftsman for an archeological team; you married, the sooner the better, some Egyptian in order to acquire Egyptian citizenship, bore a son and named him Seti. But the Seti of this present age showed no inclination to live alone with you at Abydos; he completed his medical studies and left for America, vainly trying to induce you to go with him. So you remained at Abydos with that first long-dead Seti. And your husband? He faded away, melted, as surgeon's stitches when the wound has healed.

The Department of Antiquities in Nasser's Egypt granted you a modest post as custodian of the temple at Abydos with that first long-dead Seti. And why not? For the strange English girl who lived alone on the necropolis bank of the Nile and who every morning bathed her eyes in the muddy pond above Osiris's grave was herself a tourist attraction.

I came to know many of your acquaintances; those who respected you intuitively, not understanding you, those who tittered at you with much sympathy, and those who slandered you passionately. Some were amazed at your incredible knowledge of the past Abydos and of Egypt in general, some concluded that you were a magnificent charlatan who had managed to reach the pages of the greatest newspapers of the world. But I, not knowing you, know who you are, Um Seti, for I see to whom you are betrothed; to him whom I, too, am betrothed. We know one another, by our masters, by our freedom.

* Even firmer, Um Seti, even firmer!

158

we are really searching for, you and I. For, Um Seti, great lady of Abydos, that frenzy with which we seek after truth, is it not changed, finally, into a drug without which we can no longer even walk, let alone fly? For now we could do without our life, but never without that search.*

I wanted to go to Abydos to ask you about that, but there was war and the holy city was encircled by barbed wire. Twice I tried, twice I didn't succeed. And now, as you see, I write you, for in a short time I shall leave Egypt and your Osiriana will also near its end.

I rejected question after question in the stormy pre-Misir years and in the end I came to the threshold of Misir deprived of everything save a doubt. Standing on your soil, I no longer ask is man able to become the truth for which he seeks. Now I ask if the effort of becoming truth does not derange the seeker so much that he is finally driven out of his senses if he does not succeed at the cost of terrible labor to liberate the madness that is in him. The madman is convinced that he is, let us say, a Pharaoh. He has just as much proof of that as the man of religion has for a god or the mystic for the drowning in supreme reality. The drinker of *soma* or *ayahuasca,* the devotee of Krishna or the frenzied dervish, the saint who dances for days on end or who remains motionless for days, the *maharisha* drowned in *samada,* are they not for the psychiatrists similar to their euphorics and catatonics, who are so taken up with something in themselves that they see nothing else and cannot explain to others what it is all about? God is never far distant from the devil, and the madder we are the wiser we are, my divine old lady! Look now, how the serpent's poison heals me, how for long past it has healed me in my heart; for the more I am uneasy

---

* Too fierce a thirst often misses the water hole and staggers on into the wilderness searching for a jewel. To a real master one cannot be enslaved, but to a service we have heedlessly assumed we are mercilessly enslaved.

the more I am at ease. If my crown is at peace, my roots tremble.

For two years I have been preparing to come and see you, Um Seti, and now, now when I have committed myself to this letter, I see that I had no real reason to come. The questions fall away of themselves, like dried scabs. Yes, I would have been frightened had we, searching for a Pharaoh, *grown to love our search more than him for whom we were searching.* I wanted to ask you—don't we, as do the holy mystics of mescalin, the drug that summons God, become victims of a secondary habit? Unholy addicts? Pouring out the sacramental wine, haven't we, inadvertently, become commonplace drunkards? That's the serpent in my heart which has been poisoning me for long past, that guardian which lies on the sunken treasure, God's left hand which has wrapped itself around the tree of paradise.

But, writing this letter, line by line, I begin to understand, with pious wonder, that the difference between the custodian and the treasure has become even less. Poison and remedy are the upper and lower lip of one and the same kiss, Um Seti. See how it heals, how deeply it heals in my heart; and my heart seeps through my body, my body seeps into the world in three great rivers which measure and encircle it. We are included in a strange equation, in truth; my letter to you returns to me with an answer that is older than the question.

Everything is as clear as it is given us to endure, Um Seti. Divisions are unreal, for between our souls and us, Um Seti, there exists nothing save us and our souls, and all the mists that confuse our sight are no more than the gleam of the purest Abydos diamond.

Farewell, therefore, forever! I will never come to Abydos behind the bristling wire, I will not circumvent the scarecrow-like guards and cross the mine fields to Osiris's tomb. A moment ago I understood that there is no distance that is not near, no heart that is not some asp—although, Um Seti, ignoramuses still crucify us on the cross of our differences. A moment ago I saw how fire and water halted in their stormy hatred, looking astounded at one another: so it's you! one whispers to the other someone whom they had sought from the beginning of their existence, yet he had always been there in the form of their most bitter adversary. A short time ago I saw that the great and the small pour into one another and the greater the great one and the smaller the small one the fiercer the pouring. Finally, the infinitely great and the infinitely small are of the same size; their measure is immeasurable, the only real dimension is in the soul. Between them stretches the unreal world, Satan's world of differences, the hell in which we live. The only reality, Um Seti, is that which has no frontiers, which is the soul that serves the unreal world as a frontier.

A short moment ago I saw that and the echo of that sight is lost in these sentences. Until at last I understand that the diamond that flees from me and the coal that I hold in my hand are one and the same, I will understand nothing *lasting*.

Everything is as clear as we need it to be, Um Seti. For we know nothing if we only know. We do not exist if we only exist.

THE RETURN OF THE SCARABAEUS

*Whoso becomes the owner of a scarabaeus amulet,
let him know that the lucky beetle will very soon
forsake him and will later return to him in some
unexpected manner. Scarabs are like that in their
moods. In 1962 I bought in one of the harbor shops
of Port Said a ring with a green scarab—a ring such
as today is scattered throughout the world on a
thousand fingers. It accompanied me across the
Indian Ocean to Bombay, where I lost it even before
setting foot on dry land.*

*In Egypt, in the course of those thousand days,
I didn't think of any one of those countless scarabs
as the return of my little Port Said insect. Until the
day before yesterday. Yes, but the tale is not so
straightforward.*

At the foot of the Aker-kuf ziggurat a brightly colored snake,
a poisonous snake, was lying. I passed it by with tense steps
and with a deep feeling of guilt. Probably it had slithered
out of the ditch around the ziggurat and there, at the foot
of the steps, the custodian had broken its spine with an old
Kassite brick. Had he killed it anywhere else in that region
round about us crumbling in the sun, I would not have
been so affected. As it was, it seemed to me that it, too, had
wanted to do just what I was doing—to climb up to the
temple. That desire had revealed it to its enemy.

I had not killed that snake, but I would certainly have

162

told the custodian to do so had I arrived at the Aker-kuf ziggurat an hour or two before. Ah, it is all the same who brandishes the knife or the stone; and when he does it. We always participate if we are able to feel the hate and terror of the murderer.

From my trip to Iraq I brought back one mature foreboding. Even as a man sends himself dreams, so, too, he sends himself reality; and inasmuch as the language of dreams is charged with secret messages, so, too, is the language of reality. "Why?" I thought to myself, gazing at the dead asp at the foot of the magnificent ruin. "Why plunge into dream and the language of the night when reality continually sends even clearer and simpler portents?" But we are not accustomed to pay heed to the signal and the language addressed to a conscious brain; we regard them as neither eloquent nor symbolical.

One August evening in Cairo when our hanging garden was exhaling warm steam from its green lungs, I noticed in the twilight on the floor a largish black stain; it was like a muddied onyx out of which a thin, delicate antenna had grown. I went nearer; it was quite still. It had a large, dense carapace at least three centimeters long.

(I am particularly disgusted by cockroaches, which advance irrepressibly from wastepipes and garbage cans: huge, black, light shy, they crawl everywhere by night—around the kitchen, inserting themselves into empty milk and Coca-Cola bottles and into the icebox; they lick up drops of the children's fruit juice, couple in the saucepans, and, night after night, grow fatter and more numerous. I am not disgusted by anything else; on the contrary, I have eaten food from unclean kitchens with good appetite, have drunk water from the public cups in the streets of thirsty Indian cities, have traveled in dirty ramshackle rickshaws, and have not been afraid of the mice in the students' hostel at Delhi. But I have sprinkled those cockroaches with every sort of poison, have lit smoke tablets and not even shrunk from killing them with a broom.

A few days later they would invade again; at night the kitchen would rustle with their brisk tiny feet. I have dreamed of them crawling on the wall above my bed and at such a spectacle I would waken disturbed, as if the alarm clock had gone off. I knew that I had not dreamed those cockroaches from the kitchen against which I had contended in the daylight, and knew that the daylight cockroach was the envoy of the black cockroaches of my dreams.)

The insect on the terrace was not a cockroach but it was like one. It was large and unfamiliar. I said to Radivoje, who was slumped in a bamboo easy chair, leafing through a newspaper: "There's something strange down here. Come and look."

Bored by my idiosyncrasies he rose nonchalantly; but when he got nearer the dense oval stain on the floor, he was startled: "Oho!" he said, and raised a foot to squash it.

"Don't kill it," I said, filled with anxiety. "Just throw it over the balcony."

"Why?" he muttered, looking at me indecisively. The insect remained still.

"Perhaps it isn't an insect after all," I went on with false hope.

"What else could it be? You can see it's got feelers. Obviously it's dangerous. What if it stings the children at night?"

He raised his foot and crushed the vague shape; something crunched and crackled, but did not move, only flattened. He trod on it twice more; it was hard, like a thick-shelled pod. A whitish mush oozed through its dark amor.

"Ugh!" said Radivoje. "It stinks! Let's see what it is!" He took a piece of newspaper, shoveled up the crushed insect, and brought it under the gleam of light that filtered through the sitting-room door. I drew back. I was deeply unhappy about what had happened and, like a criminal, didn't want to look at my victim. But a single stealthy glance at the dead unknown was enough for me to recognize it.

"It's a scarab!" I cried out, horrified, feeling that my eyes were shining with unshed tears. "Really! A scarab!" Radivoje said unexpectedly, gazing at the formless armor which till then we had seen only in reproductions in porcelain or gold. Then, glancing toward me and noticing my reaction, which he felt was excessive, he quickly returned to his customary factual logic: "What if it is? What's the difference between a scarab and any other beetle?"

I slipped quickly into one of the bedrooms, where my younger boy was just getting ready for bed. My heartbeats pounded through my body. It was as if I had brought suffering on a dear and valued friend. But I was not only sad; I was afraid. I shuddered and quivered. You see, reality is fantastic, reality is more irrational and more symbolic than any dream, more psychedelic than LSD, more subconscious than subconsciousness itself. Then, in my own person, I realized that I didn't need to go either to Babylon or to Machu Picchu to discern that omen of my unrevealed being. For the symbols were here, in the kitchen, on the terrace, under my husband's slippers, in the garbage can; there they lay for anyone to see, in the eye of reality.

Next morning—and that was yesterday—I cautiously approached the place of the scarab's murder. On the floor a greasy spot the shape of its body was blackening. I asked myself how the scarab—*Scarabaeus sacer* *—an insect which has long forgotten how to fly, was able to reach the tenth

* *Scarabaeus sacer* lives in the sand dunes. Its specialty is that it pastes its eggs together with earth and then rolls the little lump uphill to the summit of the dune and lets it roll down again on the far side of the ridge. It repeats that labor until, from the constant rolling up and down hill, the lump becomes so large and rounded that it serves as a safe cradle for the scarab's descendants.

Because of its mania for pushing uphill, the scarab seemed to the ancient Egyptians a sacred symbol (hieroglyph) of that energy which pushes the sun to its zenith. Here is what Anan, scribe to the Pharaoh Seti I, writes about it: "The scarab with its little feet rolls small balls into which it puts its eggs. The Egyptians consider that this is a perfect image of the Creator who pushes the world forward and ensures that it conceives life."

floor? Mama was of the opinion that the sacred beetle had in all probability been living for some time in the greenery of the terrace. Anyway, the problem of how it managed to get there in the first place remained unsolved. Our landlord, a Moslem, obviously had little interest in ancient Egyptian or Coptic superstitions. Seeing that it was so large, why hadn't we noticed it before, since we spent a good deal of our time on the terrace and knew its morning and evening voices by heart and all its colors by day or night? Since the scarab is so heavily amored, the wind could not have blown it to such a height. Whence and how had it got there, motionless as if driven from someone's dream and still not understanding that it was real and alive and that it could escape from its enemies?

I amused myself with such thoughts, with those questions that seemed so occult and so insoluble that they had been able to lure on a false trail my otherwise keen-scented police dog. But on that blistering morning my investigations got off on the wrong foot and even the dog didn't feel this chase to be worth his while.

Gradually I became aware of some conflicting signals which reached me from within. Around midday the whole investigation took another turn. It became evident that all my morning thoughts were a kind of mask behind which I had been hiding from myself. For the question how the scarab had come and gone was irrelevant, whether it had crawled up from the Lybian sand dunes or from the Mokattam quarries, whether it had crawled there by chance or had been driven by some magnetic force which began and ended in my own psyche was all the same. What was important was the moral lesson it triggered off in me, a process that had "pushed" it uphill into the focus of consciousness. The scarab, after all, was only a hieroglyph which had stimulated the archetypal center of comprehension.

Setting aside its origin, I turned back to the language of ancient times, to the language of the whole, to the language with which the Gondwana of our times asks and replies:

166

"Well, what am I to do now? I didn't know it was you. I repent. Feeling is more important than any ritual of reconciliation I could offer you. I'm sorry. What more do you want?"

A silence filled with disapproval; obviously something else was wanted. But what? The trial had only just begun.

I felt like someone who has resolutely set out to keep an appointment long ago postponed, and stopped with one foot still in the air after the first painful step. My foot was raised and under it the depths of an unknown soil. I resisted, but I had to go farther. The scarab does not sacrifice itself in vain.

The sentence I had despised last night resounded in my conscience like a revelation: "What if it is? What's the difference between a scarab and any other beetle?" Wisdom often shames us when we have turned our back on it. Yes, what difference is there? Between the sacred beetle and, let us say, a cockroach?

Everything was clear, clearer than in any interpretation of dreams by Freud or Jung. The terrace swayed; it began to swallow and to resume its outlines. It sank through the porous membrane of the day somewhere into night and unconsciousness; then suddenly rose once more into the light, splashing my transparent two-dimensional noon in the most unexpected places.

"Inasmuch as ye have done evil unto one of the least of these my brethren, ye have done it unto Me." My uneasiness began to subside; the crushed scarab became for me a symbol of love and not of bad luck. Something, redeemed, raised its head within me—the snake-martyr on the steps of the temple, a voice to which I paid no heed in the day and therefore sucked my blood by night.

"You allowed me to be crushed because you looked on me as a relative of a beetle abhorrent to you. Now perhaps you see that to be a scarab is a part of every cockroach and that with every cockroach you kill a part of holiness, a part of your happiness. I came to you in dream, disguised as fear and danger—why? Because to me you were dangerous, because I feared you; lest you suffocate me. Now perhaps you will recognize me, for I have done the greatest thing I could have done: I have sacrificed myself of my own free will."

I understood and at the same moment promised It:

"I won't, I won't ever, kill you again. Go now! Go back and push the sun."

That understanding is only the beginning of a process that is above understanding. In the transformation that I await in myself my reason can no longer help. For mechanically and rationally to refrain from killing is not enough; the heart must change. And to change the heart means to purify the heart from all disgust and poisonous fears. From all disgust, from all fear; there is not that heaven of love which could fortify itself with hatred of the devil. Yes, every man on his journey meets Christ, every man has been moved by his love, but there are few who take it so far as not to feel hatred for the enemies of Christ.

From that day—and that day was yesterday, moved to an illimitable distance—the sun appeared as something unreliable, as something that could easily plunge down on the wrong side, were it not for the scarab's help. Obviously there coursed through me the sentiments of the ancient Egyptians; they experienced the rise of the sun to the summit of the heavenly dune as a strenuous labor which called on them for their participation. Nothing in nature, they knew, is to be taken for granted, nothing happens of itself. Life is a unity where there are no insignificant participators.

From that time onward—and, in truth, it was yesterday—I felt a premonition that every day a psychic and heliocentric catastrophe is avoided only by a miracle—at the price of someone's martyrdom. Someone by his sacrifice continually averts the destruction of the world.

THE GATE OF THE HOMELAND

*The gate stands always the same, open, and below it,
tangled and twisted, the threads of the meridian . . .
they rush like a herd of horses that offer their backs
always to the same motionless rider.*

THE PROBLEM
Before the gate that I have for so long yearned to enter grows
a flower which says: "There is nothing there except me.
Don't go farther than the petal."

It is hard not to believe the flower. It seems so full of self-
confidence. A victim or a crafty Argus?

IN INDIA AND LATER
Before the gates of the great mystery grows a hundred-headed
soul-devouring flower which hunts the little fly of my attention. Before the entrance to the shrine within which grows
the bare severe axis of the cosmos, the multicolored foam
of existence splashes abundantly over me, the millionfold
movement of maya on the surface of the temple.

Before the gate of the temple which for so long I have
yearned to enter, the murmurous wave of maya which still
sustains me has splashed over me. Clearly I am not yet ready
to enter. Thus I, the unsuccessful *yogina*, instead of stretching out my arms to the heavens stretch them out to the
earth, and from the earth there spring up at once Adam

and two little Cains, and maya whirls about us on the surface of the temple of Maha Deva.

IN EGYPT AND ALWAYS

My loves, my fathers and sons, watch me through the eye of a keyhole. O dear and only refuge, O home surrounded by a high wall! Everything that I have done and which those closest to me regarded as sin or even fine work was a knocking, a test of the knocker and the latch. Like an eel with built-in memory I slither along my old tracks and turn before the House of Conception.

My life is your prodigal daughter, love. The closer I am to our home, the most I fear; lover and father, how shall I find You? Haven't my wanderings fatigued You? Will You accept me, so changed, as Your kin?

"Let me come in," I whisper, remembering the secret which I never saw with my own eyes. "Let me in through the petals, through the scorpion's claws, through the tentacles of the octopus! Over a lake with three blinding flashes strike me! Through the harshness of a male body thread me!" This is what I implored gazing into the green jaw out of which steam rose.

"Why did you come?" mother-snake asks me, iron beak asks me, dragon-shaped bud asks me.

"I came to be born, to die, O mother," I answer, and my lips grow into a reed, into a pipe, into a banquet horn; wine and fruit and songs pour out, fall beneath their feet, before their lair and their cave. Giants bow down, collect my offerings, eat and become Lilliputians, become hummingbirds and lizards.

And all these obeisances and the songs that grow on my lips like roses on a grave assume more and more the appearance, the shape, the mood, of that guardian flower. O dear and only shelter, O home whose ramparts in the clouds I raise! It is not easy to leap over oneself and not to know that you have wings.

DREAMING OF AWAKENING

Weary from the journey, I sit at the base of the city walls and sing lullabies to the dragons. Surely someone will come to awaken me? In the central palace, in a golden cradle, my father dreams a dream of his prodigal daughter who knocks at the gate of her homeland. Will you not open your eyes, O father mine, will you not see that I am a bad dream? A dream that makes still more beautiful the beauty of awakening?

THE PRINCESS AND THE CRIPPLE

The wild beasts lay, wound against wound, and whispered: "There are no wounds." And, behold, there were no wounds.

The princess and the cripple are the compost for the tree of the world, for the savor of the fruit, which half ripens, half decays. This is how it was:

Kings had sought her hand. There was not one among them who was not perfect, whose coach had not a hundred horses. Each had a pipe at the sound of which palaces built themselves. She would certainly have remained unmarried forever had there not appeared one day in the park a beggar, a cripple. Everyone gazed at him in astonishment, the princess most of all. She had never before seen a being without arms, a creature blind and crippled. Was it something more perfect than perfection? For defects attract, just as do qualities. Since he was the only cripple among so many who were perfect, she chose him.

She could scarcely persuade him to take her. He grumbled: "Those superfluous arms and legs of yours! On the journeys that I take, they mean three or four more ways to get tired and ten more false steps on top of that!" She laughed, regarding that as transoceanic wit. But when they reached the cripple-city she, too, longed to have only one arm and not a single eye.

Everyone wondered at that team, even the young couple

themselves. Why had she, so swift-footed, become the companion of a man who staggered on crutches? Why had he, prince of cripples, become the escort of a wild beast with winged hands? Hidden behind a bush, she watched him and tried to resolve the riddle of his cryptic stumbling, which was like the trail of a lame raven. Perhaps it was a matter of a letter—of concentric letters to be read from the perspective of a bird? Perhaps he would in the end impale her on his beggar's staff? Or perhaps at midnight he would strip off his beggar's appearance and become a king's son, without equal among the best.

Years flew by and many roads passed under their feet. One day he cried: "Ow! I have a thorn in my heel!" and crouched on his withered legs till she calmly took a thorn out of her own heel. Then it happened that she awoke, leaning on his crippled shoulder; on their journeys she limped along beside him, hanging to his dislocated joints. So one day he said to her: "Would you like me to lend you my hump? For this region is dangerously humpbacked and you will not pass in safety walking upright."

More and more often they lent one another some little thing or other, until they became so confused that they no longer knew what was whose. One could tell by now that the princess and the cripple were two bad halves of one sound apple; one unbearably sour and one unbearably sweet. And then, leaning against one another, they began to open veins and arteries and to pour one into the other. It was a true marriage, *conniunctio oppositorum,* under the vault of the great retorts.

(I don't know, sister, why that seems strange to you, why her choice seems stranger than his. He didn't limp any worse than she. And he was standing behind a bush, copying the hieroglyphs of her feverish flights and returns, in the foolish hope that in that script are hidden the indications of how to find a buried treasure. Ah, let's avoid false wonder. Only one question is worth asking: who is the one who separated this pair of eternal lovers, sweetness and bitterness, who bit off the cripple's arms and legs, chewed them up and then spat out the princess's wings?)

The cripple and the princess will evaporate in the answer and will not let us know the result of the experiment.

In a given space where the bottom is earth and the sky the cover, they smoke fiercely like a moist flame and the steam whirling about them assumes the face of the world at the day of creation.

That is how it was.

In the tangled roots of our garden Tristan and Isolde are buried. In the darkness of that tangle the drowsy egg of the sun travels its path and the arrogant comet, the seed of the pirate region, pierces its eardrum and awakens it. In the divided embryo grow the eternal twins, Isis and Osiris, the princess and the cripple.

Apple of the world, for whom do you ripen, for whom do we decay?

MALUS ANGELUS

In the entrails of the maiden danced a hungry urn:
go and feed it, that even my love may sleep satiated.

When I entered the arena, helmeted and in full armor, spear in hand and wearing a magic belt, I longed for one of the knights to conquer me, since, lonely and living as I was, life was unbearable to me. I prayed to God that I should be dead yet belong to someone. Like those fortunate ladies in their towers who wave silken handkerchiefs and in whose eyes is thus preserved everything that looks at them: men, heaven, children. To the end, and perhaps even beyond that.

To be dead, more than dead and still more than dead; it was that I begged from the gods. I didn't look to see who was drawing nearer to me from the other side, or whose name they called out. I was afraid to desire any one of them; I only wanted someone to conquer me, no matter who.

Always it was that same sound of feet, that same rattling of iron, that same dark shadow which the declining sun threw at my feet. Always across that shadow fell another, denser, shadow, like a sword that cut through my hope; the shadow of uninvited Lohengrin. He stood upright between us like an Icelandic geyser, the symbol of my maiden island; I knew what he would say, so many times had I heard his challenge:

175

"He who wants to conquer her must first conquer me."

I know, I know, he is *my* shadow. I adore the fire of those who attack him, I love their vain bravery. Later, I collect their fragments, which seem to have been scattered by a mighty tempest. I stick them together, I sew them, I stuff them with my hair. In that task I probably mingle limbs and bodies. Lohengrin has vanished; he has once more entered into me, longing for yet one more victory. He has laid waste the mighty citadel, he has left the widowed star prostrate on the battlefield; his harness clangs with a rusty sound in the antique cabinet.

That was all, that was all that took place between us, my noble knights. I squandered my youth, allowing that crafty beast which I placed before the entry to my cage to torture you. You went away, ill-fashioned and patched up, you went back to your ladies, in whose eyes you will once more become whole, and to whose loyalty it is too little to be merely a mirror. They will add to you twofold all that I took from you. You have gone and the beast has remained, an image of darkness crouched before the exit from my loneliness.

How long shall we go on like this, beast, father, Lohengrin? What do you intend to do with me if you don't intend to free me? How long shall we be to one another the whole conversation and the whole weariness of it? All wealth and all deprivation?

Listen, high above the tower unravels the plaited braid of whiplashes and the winds like snakes whirl through the ribs and the homes. We listen in the cellars, among the amphoras of wedding wine whose seals bear the invisible escutcheon of the bridegroom. The red vineyards on the slopes of blood are withered, far away in the world; buried in memory of sunken treasure about which our descendants dream. A map showing the way there hangs on the wall behind my back, but I am sitting so that I cannot turn my head. Instead, I gaze at the back of my keeper, on which the darkness has tattooed its indecipherable runes.

Yes, yes, in the depths of the towers and the churches the amphoras ferment with hymeneal wine, there, there! And through the multitudes in the cities above flows the scent of incomprehensible orgy; it begins to sway like a treasure ship, and so, too, sway the stones of the high ramparts, the towers fluttering like ribbons in the clouds, the balconies flying like swings in the springtide. Bells can be heard; it is holiday; I go out for a walk amid the joyous crowd but on one leg I drag behind me the chain from the subterranean womb. O it is unbearable that I am no one's and yet so many times born! Let me be dead and someone's forever; that is what I implore from God. Like those happy ladies about the battlefield.

Yes, yes, in the depths of the towers and the churches, where ferment the amphoras filled with hymeneal wine, where I come forth when the year transgresses. Helmeted, in armor, with my spear and a twofold shadow.

How long will it be like this, Beowulf, Marius, Lohengrin? How glad I would be to see your blood, *vinum ardens,* sealed with the seal of the Unknown. I don't know who you are, I don't know you, but I have the feeling that we are skewered on the same beam of light.

THE PURUSHA SIDE OF THE WORLD

A hundred fish set out to search for the Hundred-fish.
Paraphrase of a Sufi metaphor

One July afternoon, when the Cairo day swelled up like bread in an oven, I, thinking of nothing at all, bit into the tail of some beginning which rose dancing from the Ocean of Unwritten Texts. It could have been the tail of some quivering flying fish or a nonpoisonous snake. Without real curiosity, weighed down by the oppressive day, I gulped down an invitation to plunge.

I didn't have time to regret. All of a sudden I lost my breath—the monster, for it was a monster, dived headlong into the depths and dragged me under my own skin.

Of the seven sides of the world only one is real and leads to existence, whereas six are unreal and lead to nonexistence. That one, that seventh one, leads to man—by a long and unaccustomed path. The remaining six lead outside man into a sixfold external world to which our eyes and ears are turned. Now, evidently, we were rushing along that seventh side of the world.

I had no time to look upward and call for help from that burning belly which I now saw from within; like the swollen cupola of Mother Nut to the wall of which fitted snugly a tiny egglike planet tumultuously swaying.

I had no time for the evil things and monsters surrounding me, whetting their barbs and spines, and which, it was obvious, had long been awaiting me. I had not suspected how many terrible beasts I had nourished under my skin, how many animals from primeval times, winged scorpions, a dark lair of horror. The lonely candle of my brain did not manage to illuminate it. Hideous fish from the subconscious broke away from the cliffs of darkness to rush toward the faint gleam which swung on that sea of shadow.

Nevertheless, the deeper we fell, the pleasanter the phantoms became, the tamer the birds of prey. The farther we moved away, the larger I grew and the smaller my guide became. I became greater, stronger, denser. Leviathans began to play about me like goldfish. The circle of the horizon collapsed like a punctured balloon and everything that was in it was compressed into a single breath, the breath I was breathing.

Now I was alone and motionless. I received the sacrament of the seventh direction, swallowed it and ceased to advance. On my palm trembled the world—slimy and egg-shaped. When this, too, evaporated, I was transformed into a cosmic monster, into Purusha.

Afterward, I don't know how many eons afterward, I wanted not to be alone; so I divided myself into billions. Every particle of my being longed to go outside me. It occurred to one among the billions to move along the seventh side of the world. One only among billions succeeded in plunging into the abyss, to rush through the awe-inspiring guardians. That single one began to grow and devour its father, the primordial giant, until it had swallowed it to the last fragment and itself became Purusha; thus it fastened a fresh link on the chain of the worlds.

When I regained my breath, six worried hands awaited me and tapped me on the cheek. Oh! Dear One, unreal old face! For billions of centuries I had not seen it. They surround me, they whisper: "For a moment you were not among us."

ASTRAL JOURNEY

Kosjenka is the shadow of my body. Every night she rides the black horse of dream, herself white, so white that through her one sees its pitch-black mane. The Bujan path flashes with lightning, on Alatir she sits, Kosjenka, fairy shadow.

The hills of lightning show through her as she rides the roaring storm in the saddle of her gloomy steed. She melts away from the chain of my body and mounts her good black horse of dream, Kosjenka, my shadow.

Where have you been, Kosjenka, where are you going? I rode on the winged whale of Lokrum, I took my seat on Alatir, on the white rock. Where I intend to go, I tell no one.

What did you see on your journey, Kosjenka, my shadow, what have you brought me from along your way? That stone, that Alatir, whitens, whitens so intensely that it cannot be seen with the eyes. That flame, that Alatir, shimmers like pure vision: white, too white. And what I have brought to you, you cannot see with your eyes.

Ay, Kosjenka, what is your name, Kosjenka? I'm called your shadow, your shadow in the moonlight, shadowless in the sun.

Thus every night from the chain of my body the fairy shadow slips on the black horse of dream, my sister, white Kosjenka. Every night my body implores, the sluggish limping Regoč: "Take me, dear little Kosjenka, two or three fairy miles at least on your little ship of clover. Take me along

180

the moon's path on a broomstick of scented mint." My dearest fairy shadow is all laughter, laughing and twining like a drift of pearls, tickling the silver chain that links us. The black horse under her whinnies in delight.

The body sleeps but the heart keeps vigil. From it springs a tree of pearls, in that tree beats the eternal clock and on its top nests the firebird. Come in, play, the serpent sleeps and my heart, your trusty source, keeps vigil. And she laughs, laughs like a drift of pearls, and the silver lock and chain tickles. The black horse under her whinnies in delight.

Little Kosjenka, little shadow, jeweled sister of dream, harvest firefly, little St. John's Day fire, stretch out your shadow hand to me, pour out the blackberry wine from your tiny finger, bring me to Srdj under the glitter of the cross; carve my image in a switch of maple as a sign of your fairyhood on the four horseshoes of dream.

I conjure you by the black berries and the white hawthorn; keep me in mind when the sun goes down! Let your shadow be dewy and thrice transparent: let the moonlight dolphins succor you with their milk: keep me in mind when the sun goes down!

I swear by the blackthorn and the white hawthorn, let the forked-tongued serpent turn me into a snake, let me be twisted into a willow, let me be speckled in the rainbow, let me never be called your shadow or your sparkling dew. I cannot go farther with you, for I'm without shadow in the sun, for I am an unwanted woman in a world without dreams.

Look, on the threshold of the dawn glides my black horse through the gate of light, the clattering lock and chain sound the alarm and I, with the last effort of my dream, drink to the dregs the waters of Lethe.

A LEAF FROM A
TREE NAMED YGGDRASILL

Gently, too gently, a card flutters from the high, slow hands; as it falls, it falls as if it were not falling, falls as if it were dreaming that it is falling; far down to me it dreams, it falls. Dumb card, a tiny leaf from the grey trunk of Yggdrasill; down here its name is: Son.

Perhaps it fell long ago, but only now I saw it. How long have the starry ones been playing cards above my head! And how many times have I fallen asleep, not waiting for the end of the game! And now, once more awake, I see: my card falls, like a leaflet from a grey sun. Down here its name is: Son.

Now dreamed, now as if in vision, an unknown invitation lies on the card table; on it are the fingerprints of Antares, the marks of the Scorpion's claws. On its face is my face: a sign in a game which has probably finished up there above. Here below is the trump with which the game opened.

Now submissively, too submissively, I raise my Son and with Him as a pass I step onto the threshold of spring, onto the threshold of my heart. Protected from evil spells, deep in myself: I dream, I fall.

From high above trickle the leaves of the silvered Ash; in the heavens it is Fall, the crowns of the Ash wither. Here below, that is called: blessing and the budding of leaves.

RIDDLE FOR TWO BOYS

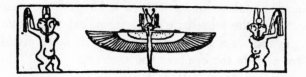

Two and a half peacocks and one whole snake will share with you the air bubble at the bottom of the ocean.

Two and a half snakes and one whole heron will be your guests in a drop of water in the entrails of the desert.

Nonetheless, my child, there is no better offer for those who wish to be born.

Six ropes and seven death rattles will embrace you in the midst of the gorge through which you rush to the mouth of the womb; six and seven will embrace you, thirteen seals will strengthen old agreements between noose and mandragora.

Even so, my child, there is no better offer for those who want to be loved.

A king's span and a cripple's ell will stay crossed on your threshold until dawn; and you will be bound to wait in the house and whenever one masters the other you will be grown by a span or be diminished by an ell.

Even so, my child, there is no better offer for those who want to struggle.

It's dawn, mother—O, how tired I am!—what is dawn? Dawn, my child, is a coral palace and in the palace a feast of amber and in the feast a goblet of crystal and in the goblet an eye—filled with tears.

Wherever it looks, there is healing.

Before it you will come sometimes in a coffin and sometimes in a cradle, sometimes as balm and sometimes as poison.

From the coral palace will stroll out half a baboon and a three-headed snake, three fingers of a king on the stump of a cripple. On the whetstone of water naked thirst sharpens its tongue and waits for your throat. But don't be afraid any more, for already the eye sees you

that heals whatever it looks at.

Then you will forget that you spent the night in the world: king and cripple, peacock and snake, death rattle and rope; that you fell on the mouth of the womb like a blind, slimy tear. And you will remember that every tear shapes the eye *which sees joy.*

Till we meet again, my tear, till we meet again, in the eye of joy!

HIDE-AND-SEEK

In the beginning there was a peak. Later, ridges and foot-hills descended. On the peak there was a clearing and on the clearing little Kosjenka walked. For only someone as mild as Kosjenka walked in our childhood and sowed here a lark, here a cornel, and there the game of hide-and-seek. Only Kosjenka's tiny pearls rustled in the clover, in the eyes of the intimate, familiar four-leaf clover.

In the beginning there was a peak and from it later descended roots, and with the roots came earth and its dark threat. Yes, the best of all had first been offered, without haggling and without wise counsels: thus are its leaves offered to the tree. The beginning of life was the peak of life; on that peak I one day awakened, immense, eternal. Yes, I was the greatest in the beginning.

Kosjenka throws a pearl and the children in a circle, like the eyes of the meadow, whirl and spin toward the sky. Kosjenka throws a second pearl and Auntie Petka bakes a cake of St. John's bread, for a holiday, for a happy beginning. Kosjenka throws a third pearl and in the eddies under the boats fairies begin to sing. Kosjenka does not throw a fourth pearl and down there in the valley dwarfs rush out, like wingless insects. Kosjenka does not throw a fifth pearl and I long to slip down the steep slope, down the mountainside, to become a dwarf, to pick up a beggar's staff. Kosjenka doesn't throw a sixth pearl and I yearn for a cake not made of St. John's bread, cooked by no auntie and not for any holiday.

Thus the leaves are deprived of their trunk; without forgiveness, without anger. Now, above, Kosjenka crumbles an unthrown pearl and I array myself, thread the necklace and tinkle my bracelets; the valley around me shines and echoes. I fast on days that are not Lenten, on holidays I feast on no St. John's bread. For such is the game to which my withering is destined. O, my prince Svarožić, this is a sad crowd but I have no choice; here I must take my part in a witches' sabbath; here I must play my restless game of hide-and-seek. Such is the game in which it is my turn to hide.

O time of pearls, where are you? I shed my tears for this wretched hiding which has already lasted too long; down here below, shadows and grey hairs have already found me and my brothers still have their eyes closed to count me out. Hurry, Svarožić, for the wrinkles come more quickly to my face and the shudders to my heart, for the herd of hungry cities stampedes and hates. And I hurry under the mountain dreaming that I shall climb by the power of my breath by the bloodstained rope. Never have there been such mad hopes!

From pearl to pearl, how many have not been pearls? There is my life, my whole life, my only life. Remember, Kosjenka, your game is eternal and countless but my breath is short and all alone. Remember me, Kosjenka, and throw the seventh pearl.

FAIRY TALE

If you set out on a search for the golden apples stolen from the tree in front of the palace or on the trail of the fire-feathers, you will one day wander to the temple of Edfu in Upper Egypt. In the temple courtyard the granite falcon, the sum of all the flights of the world, will await you.

I set out in quest of the golden apples, I left to search for the fire-feathers, and three times found myself in the region around Edfu. I started to find the shadow of the firebird and three times did not get to Edfu, three times did not get my gold. Whoever goes to Egypt will come to know the world but he who penetrates to the height of Egypt, to Edfu, will be moved to the depths of his soul.

Before my white palace grows a scarlet tree, its red crown flashing with my blood: it strikes with its quiet leaves against the chill and dark. The darkness clears and allows the most brilliant entry of the Egyptian falcon. In the dawn it gilds my palace, it gilds the apples on the branches. In the morning, when I awake in my own ashes, I see: my palace is sooty, its grass scorched.

I rise to go in search of the golden apples, I stumble after the phoenix song and the golden-fleeced Garuda phantom. Above me rolls the utmost eye, the eye fallen from the falcon's head; its pupil widens and from it rage out the glass phalluses which hiss at us and whip us, poor naked wretches, like angry snakes. When I find myself close to Edfu I halt and go no farther. For he who climbs to heaven will recognize when he is there; but he who climbs to the height of heaven will know that he is in the depths of hell.

For your eyes, for your voice, I become blind, I become deaf, O firebird, wet nurse to the fruit of my blood! I am following you, I am following myself; in the world there is no longer any third. The sun has burned out, the whips are cold. And now I can see: I wore myself out, like a road lying beneath my feet. I wasted my lips, giving myself to them as a kiss; and now, only now, am I indestructible, only now I travel, only now I love. Here, I am near your nest. I halt, I see, in the world there is no longer any other.

Edfu is no longer before me, nor is it behind me; it is neither above nor below, to right or to left of me; yet there is more of it than ever before. I have neither gone nor arrived, I am here, I have always been here. O more than always, more than never: now, now.

Frightened, I return in the direction I came from. I return where I am again two and where I am three; where my kiss is divided into many kisses and where dream, that winged bloodsucker, lures me along the same aimless eternal path.

Edfu is again firmly behind me. My arms are again safely empty. I turn and the more I turn the more golden are the soles of my feet, the more mature and ardent the heart within me. And when I find myself near to my palace, I see: the tree flames, once more unpicked. My own blood whispers to me as it comes to meet me.

SONG OF THE SPIRAL TOWER AT SAMARA

As I climb, the earth turns about in the depths below, twists around the tower like a wheel about its hub. The more I wind upward, the more swiftly we leave it behind; our carriage rushes upward with one wheel over the abyss, and, look, to the west the wheel of another fugitive grows golden, and above the trail whistles the invisible whip of the driver.

In what race are we harnessed, Samara, what is it we saw behind us, what is it we saw before us, that we rush on so madly? But the higher the climb, the more and more this journey becomes an imprint of your dizziness, my soul.

As I climb, bit by bit I shed myself, with fear and with delight; year after year, sense after sense, I cast into silence. Only my heart cries out, guiding its liberation.

For time is at our heels, O song, in a tongue which devours itself; time, clairvoyant bird, is advancing, crawling blindly like a snail. The spirit of clear speech is the ether of height in which petty singers cannot survive. As I approach the summit, the path totters and there is no longer room on it for a guide or for anyone's footsteps. For no footprints remain on the glowing embers so that I don't know if I am ascending the tower for the first time or if I have already done so countless times before. Nether and nethermost rise within me and I flee to reach the top before them. The ferment of the dark wine runs through me in a spiral whirlpool and the more I descend into myself the more my dizziness is the imprint of your ascent, my soul.

Ah, my soul, you dark red wine, it is time that we drink each other.

MYSTERIUM TREMENDUM

We stand before a strange bleak hill, tense as before the start of a duel. "It's not a hill," say some from the confused gloom. "It's a cloud." No matter what it is, it is opaque. We stretch out our hands; we try to touch it: nothing. "An optical illusion," fresh voices announce. We move to the attack, we move to embrace it, but we are always in the same place. We charge, and not one of us moves from his place. The hill is always the same distance from us. The cloud is always equally far. The illusion is always equally far.

We stop to consider and send a sound to explore; it is thrown back at us as if from a cliff and the sound returns to us strange, scarcely audible. We send a thought, as the wisest of interrogators. It touches something in the darkness, shudders as if from a blow and returns to us without an answer, dejected. After that we throw a word and the word returns to us still more swiftly and without explanation, dumb; it embraces another word, whispers in its ear, and that second word at once embraces a third, turns its head under its armpit, and all remain enigmatic, mixed up. We watch uneasily and without understanding. What does it mean? Why do our envoys behave so strangely? We send one and another returns. Infected by unknown germs.

Is there anything else to be sent to the hill? we ask in the voice of an emperor seeking a champion. Within us a bone makes itself heard, cries out in a white voice to be let out.

With all its strength it wants to cast off its veils, to bare itself before the hill, to begin to dance like a priestess. No, not you, our daughter, we whisper in horror. Is there anything else? We don't let our bone go.

Our muscles, too, ache as it schemes within. Our body, our life, aches as it lustfully plots within.

LAMENT FOR JARILO

O, Jarilo, Jarilo, how we wept for you! We wept with anger and we wept with delight, for there was no greater sorrow than to see you torn to pieces for Communion and no greater joy than to roll with you on the great Slav steppes. Later, we used to sit under the birches to bless you like pious she wolves, our limbs still weak from the holy rubbing. O, Jarilo, Tammuz, Osiris, there was never anything living on earth more insatiate than our womb; only the grave was still able to keep step with it.

O, Jarilo, Jarilo, you rode on a white horse and your crown of wheatears swayed over the fields. The noose of the year was about your neck—the stars in heaven and our kolo, our round dance, on the earth tightened it. Our dance is the surge of the wine in the banquet jug, the heavy, dense movement that travels from the vineyard slopes and evaporates in the plaited thought of a poet. We rock the cradle of the son of our Jarilo in the wheat field, we sing a lullaby while our father's flesh still stings on the palate.

Writing of you, don't I lick my own bones, taking them one by one from the heap that obscures my sight—so great is it? Was there an altar here or was it the graveyard of my herd? Or did I descend into the underworld in search of my song? Above my head throbs the sound of hoofs—here it is, over the horse without Jarilo, the crown without a head, the land without a ruler.

O, Jarilo, how happy was that time when we wept for you! How oppressive this arid century, this time of parched laments between which we, filled with brisk and vain curiosity, adore ancient peasant idols. How joyful were our fervent outbursts under the birches! How deadly the rustling in the dried wheat of blood which snaps without awaiting its finest loss: its fruit, its overheavy ear, bending in immortal seed.

POEM ABOUT CREATION

Without knowing it I embraced myself, and looking long, long, into the stranger's eyes, I began through them to discern the outlines of mountains and rivers on which I would live from now on. And I understood the murmur of countless tongues and the songs and the laments and the roar of cities, and I saw processions in which I would become many persons and so many flowers and beds for which I would so joyously grow smaller. And not knowing to whom I was speaking, I said to him:

"For all this I thank You; all treasures and all enjoyments which compel me one day to free myself from them. But before I do that, I would like to hang Your name as a bell over the valley—speak, therefore, and tell me who You are!"

And not knowing what I was doing, I bent over the stranger's lips to drink from them that life-giving name, I bent over his eyes in which I was divided into all things seen. His lips yielded under mine and sank deeper and deeper, bending me into a circle without light until I saw my own back in flight and he slid away into the womb from which I had fallen—into the mouth with which I had summoned him. And outside a word spurted forth, freed from my circle. But I, spurred by his departure, hurried still faster after those lips which drew me even deeper into that embrace without light. And whenever my lips closed the stranger's circle, one word freed itself from them. But I, scourged by their disloyalty, even more fiercely followed his trail in the gloom.

Lips which, not knowing, drove away their own kiss.

FRUCTUS VITAE

Stem of my day, the shade thrown by the trunk of night. Shade in three forests, in a thousand scents. The upright sap bears the crown of my words, the garden of my singing; that is the echo of the unseen trunk which grows in my silence, in the divine ear. Yes, brilliance of my wakening, that is the shadow of my dream.

In the tree, in the shade of the tree, one nest, the shadow of one nest, one bird, the shadow of one bird. A bird's eye and sight are one and the same virgin dew, the mutual reflection of the jewel of my sight.

I wait for those two birds to grow uneasy and fly away, each to a different tree, to lose their trail in the egg that is the essence of all eggs. I wait for the real pollen to dust the shadow of a bud, I thirst for the taste of the fruit that will come in time. And while I evoke the marvel of that conception I don't notice that one and the same twittering knocks at both trees.

I am getting ready to leave, and someone is continually hurrying me, delaying me. I have no time to see who it is. But I say to him: "Don't hurry me, because I cannot be late. Don't delay me, for I cannot arrive too early." Ah, if only we knew what we are getting ready for while we are getting ready.

I am restless; I seem to have forgotten something important. I count everything, time and again. I go into the garden, into the street, into the children's room, into the spare room; I stand before the house door; on the square, before the shop window, I wait, I make ready. Yet something always rustles around me, dogs my steps and will not let me remember. And I have no time to look and see what it is.

That day, yes that day, everything was as it had been on any other day. Only I stamped more heavily on the earth and it opened under my feet; it happened that I struck the right spot, for someone at once called from below. But before I plunged down, I looked at him to call out a last good-bye. My fall was halted and I whispered despairingly: "Can it be You?" and wanted to leap out of the pit but your laughter smothered me. Your hearty laugh, the thud of burial.

I am getting ready to leave and someone keeps on hurrying me, delaying me. Ah, if only we knew what we are getting ready for while we are getting ready. What have I forgotten and who is it who will not let me remember? He dogs my steps. whispers in my ear, but I have no time for that dear rustling. I am always getting ready, always forgetting to look about me.

LITANIES FOR THE SOUL

My soul which art in heaven
Thy kingdom come, above and below,
My soul which is both.

Sometimes there is nothing between you and me, and sometimes there is a universe of heterogeneous beings. Ever since
I first had any memory of myself, I have swallowed the dark
waters that divide us, ever since I can remember, a clear
drop is all my thirst.

My soul, O Bengal cicada, you are the holy insect to which
nothing is sufficient; neither pleasure nor suffering. I am
your painful, mindless shrilling.

I swallow the dark waters, O atoll ringed by skerries which
hem you in like the ring of the womb when it encloses the
seed within itself! Show me a gorge where one passes by a
fanged reef into a lagoon; tell me when the fiery dragon
drowses over the treasure in the lake. Defend me from its
guardian which becomes ever more furious, ever stronger,
the nearer I approach.

> O my soul, defend me,
> My soul, do not forsake me!
> Soul, soul, do not deliver me
> To your archenemy!

Between you and me there is nothing except you and me;

but I, ever since I existed, squander the alien space between us. By doing so, I enrage it and provoke it. Defend me from evil maelstroms in the depths of heaven, from black pits that swirl under the footsteps of the angels, defend me from my shadow which behind my back whets its knife!

Ha, bloodsucker, for how long have you been emptying me, your chalice, and in the breathing spell singing a toast; I hear you thundering on high in a voice as from a whirlwind. For a long time, little bear, you have carried me in your jaws, looking around for some quiet corner, occupied— by what? By the summits of hunger or the summits of love?

O soul, soul, what have you decided? Can you in any way change your mind?

Without my eyes you are darkness, and with my eyes you are a light that blinds me. Don't let me speak to you any more but take me to yourself and shut me in, enclose me like a kolo around a St. John's Day bonfire. Don't let me exist any longer, close around me like a ring around someone's finger.

> My soul, I am your malady
> and crucifixion.
> Carry me to the summit,
> by the crossroads nail me
> four times.
> Drink me down, a destined chalice,
> O drunkard soul,
> I am the dregs of your thirst.

ASKING RIDDLES

We shall arrive when we cease to travel.

Water comes to water, asking for water—what is it?

Be where you are and be whatever you are. Otherwise don't exist and nothing else exists. That's that.

I seek You, I seek You so much; therein lies the danger that I don't find You. Searching for You, I create Your absence. He whom I search for in the unknown—what is He? Those six wise brothers don't win the kingdom; for it is the seventh, simple-minded, brother who wins it. That's that.

The farthest is nearest, the most unattainable is what you already own. There is nothing farther, there is nothing more difficult. That's that.

See, the water which, thirsty, comes to the water, not knowing that it is water. What is is, that is what. Neither question nor answer: that's that.

CONCLUSION TO A BIOGRAPHY

Whose face are you, tell me, one and only face?
You are mine, in my loves, in my pains,
    as is the rose in its petals.
Whose face are you, tell me, O beloved face?
Let me see you one last, endless, time.

I set out to touch my little life, and all of a sudden it grew larger and moved away from me with great strides, turning its back on me. Following it, coughing in the cloud of golden dust, I regretted my carelessness. But how otherwise could I have learned that I am that chosen fruit, that shell from which I could resolve to extract the kernel of my life? I believed that that was my task; yet it was life that spat me out onto the road at the point when I believed that I was about to bite the core of the fruit.

But so it should be; life should have taught me sense, to rid itself of me. While doing so perhaps I might have succeeded in seeing its face and then perhaps I would have seen that we don't differ.

LET US BREATHE OUR LAST
WITH A POEM

I recalled in dream all my awakening and remembered even more than had been. In waking I forgot all that I had dreamed, forgot even more than I had dreamed. For all that, I was never either more or less, but always just the same.

The breath of this record grows shorter and shorter. I have no time to write at greater length, with the usual superfluity. Surely our end is drawing near; let us breathe our last with a poem, O my understanding, with crystal-clear fragments of the first sun. I wrote for seven months, trying to find my own trail. All that time I had been writing just as I had been living; without compulsion, submissively listening to the voices of the demons summoning me from behind corners which I never succeeded in turning. I wrote without tension, either to complete my experience or perfect my writing. Without intention to swim out into some recognizable literary form, to strain for some enigmatic conclusion, to maintain any unity of style or method. If this book has any value, then its value is in the swirling of enchanted whirlpools, unable to clarify either its future name or form. Because of that it might remind one of all that takes place in the depths of the cosmos, in the depths of the psyche. That day of all days, that seventh day, has not yet dawned for us, my understanding, and therefore we are not capable of creating anything which dares to call itself a *magnum opus*; we are only capable of trying.

For seven months the language of poetry contended with the false convention of the truth of storytelling, for seven months the language of poetry grew through the threadbare weave of prose thought. For that language does not comprehend the satisfaction of storytelling; where one is serene the other is restless, where one glorifies the other smothers, where one arrives the other begins. I wanted to disclose the innerness of my life, but I quickly realized that the "innerness" of life cannot be "disclosed" if it is not first trimmed on all sides. Gradually and without premeditation I rejected storytelling and reached a region of dazzling lack of understanding where language melts and its joints and corpuscles become deceptively loosened and from its flicks and glows are formed the emblems of a new state of mind. Thus I reached a region which I had earlier predicted: a starting point. But what I brought from my trip has transformed that starting into a final haven.

As always, by poetry I penetrate into the unfulfilment by which my life is both wounded and blessed. Wounded: for Krishna's heartlessness alone does not make one weary. Blessed for, as you see, my chalice sings:

It is more joyous to thirst for you, O ancient wine, than to be filled with some weak and tasteless drink. I am richer empty of you than filled to the brim with the strongest alien liquor.

In the desire to touch the seed from which I grow . . . I crouch and twist my joints in pain. This book bears witness to the fakir spirit, the flower that stands on the shoulder of the inner sun and by its force believes that the great sphere of heaven is only a spark of that subterranean fire.

In the desire to touch the silence from which I speak . . . I speak. With lips, with pen. I pass through the guard of honor which stands around the sarcophagus where lies the only unplundered corpse of our history: the diamond Pharaoh illuminates the darkness of our tomb.